STALKED by SPIRITS

About the Author

Vivian Campbell is a second-generation Floridian, born in Orlando a good decade before King Mickey Mouse cemented over a lovely swampy orange grove on the outskirts of town. Dubbed a "Ghost Magnet" for her ability to mind her own business and still have spooks tapping on her shoulder, Vivian grew up and has lived in haunted houses from Tennessee to Georgia to Florida. She enjoys locating supernatural entities for historical tour groups, authors, and curious residents. A few of her experiences (under her real name) have been included in the book *Oldest Ghosts* by Karen Harvey, and the books *Ancient City Hauntings: More Ghosts of St. Augustine* and *Ghost Hunting in Florida*, both by Dave Lapham. In 2003, Tours St. Augustine based one of their nightly ghost tours, entitled *Shadows of the Past*, on some of her ghost investigations in America's oldest city. Vivian's spirit-sensing abilities were featured during a documented haunting investigation of the St. Francis Inn in the 2005 "Haunted Houses" segment of Turner South's *Blue Ribbon* television series.

Vivian and her family—along with many of the same ghosts—still live in the creepy, creaky, sometimes cranky, but very beloved five-generation Orlando home in this book.

VIVIAN CAMPBELL

STALKED
by
SPIRITS

true tales of a ghost magnet

Llewellyn Publications
Woodbury, Minnesota

FIRST EDITION
First Printing, 2012

Book design by Bob Gaul
Cover art: Girl © iStockphoto.com/Jake Holmes
         Door © iStockphoto.com/Shaun Low
Cover design and illustration by Kevin R. Brown
Editing by Nicole Edman
Interior Art: Family Tree © Llewellyn Art Department

Llewellyn Publications is a registered trademark of Llewellyn Worldwide Ltd.

Library of Congress Cataloging-in-Publication Data
Campbell, Vivian, 1961–
  Stalked by spirits: true tales of a ghost magnet/by Vivian Campbell.—1st ed.
    p. cm.
  ISBN 978-0-7387-2731-8
1. Ghosts—United States. 2. Haunted places—United States. I. Title.
  BF1472.U6C3535 2012
  133.1092—dc23
  [B]
                        2011034470

Llewellyn Publications
A Division of Llewellyn Worldwide Ltd.
2143 Wooddale Drive
Woodbury, MN 55125-2989
www.llewellyn.com

Printed in the United States of America

/ 33. 1
  C

Dedication

This book is dedicated with deep love to my precious children, Ian, Erin, and Elise; to my very wonderful mother, Jeanette, now born into heavenly eternity; and to all those—past and present—who love this house.

Contents

Acknowledgments

Countless thanks are due to many people: To my dad, for bringing our family lineage to life through his detailed genealogical research. To my late and very dear grandparents, for passing their magical house on to me. To my great friends author Dave and Sue Lapham, for their encouragement, inspiration, editorial tips, and really fun ghost-hunting trips. To my treasured comrade and confidante Nancy, for motivating me through her talented writing, editing suggestions, brandy sangria, laughter, and midnight ghost walks. And to my life-long pals who are the sisters I never had: Susie, Cathy, Haley, Dawn, Manjusha, Lisa, Mary, Sally, Lisa, Eva, Pam, Jeanne, Claire, Scott and Shelly, and author Karen Harvey, for always believing in me, despite my ghosts.

Author's Note

Some names have been changed in order to protect the privacy of certain individuals detailed in this true text.

> *Some hang above the tombs,*
> *Some weep in empty rooms,*
> *I, when the iris blooms,*
> *Remember.*
> —Mary Elizabeth Coleridge, "On Such a Day"

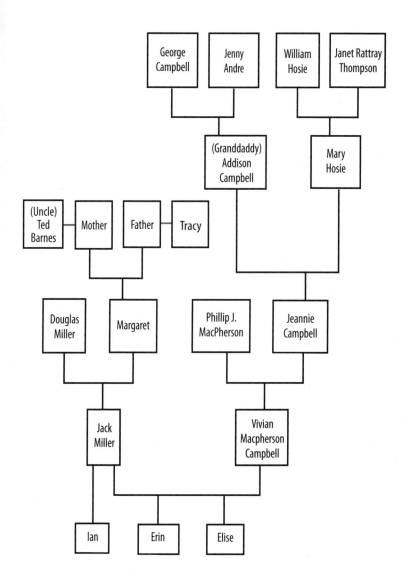

INTRODUCTION

It was the fall of 2003, and the stylish young gent from the turn of the century—the twentieth century, that is—turned his head at an impossible angle and sneered. Lurking by his side, a massive wolf shook its matted gray coat to emphasize its master's words, then sat silently on its haunches. Slowly turning its head, the beast fixed its glowing eyes, white hot with hatred, on my husband, Jack.

Frozen with horror, Jack managed one slow step backward under the open door frame that barely separated him from the demonic pair. Just moments before, he had been snoozing in his comfy, sky-blue recliner while yet another episode of *I Love Lucy* droned from the TV at his feet. Suddenly, Jack's brain screamed with pain as dozens of grizzled hands smashed into his shoulders, crushing and ripping like razors trying to slice through bread dough. His torso was wildly flung back and forth;

his sleepy head flopped like a shaken newborn. Jack's terrified eyes were wide open, his flailing hands clutched frantically at seemingly empty air. Where were the sadists who were beating him like a rag doll?

Adrenaline finally kicked in. Jack sprang from his chair of torture and staggered to the nearby door frame that separated the dining and front rooms. His nails dug into the dark woodwork as he weakly leaned against the opened door. His right wrist throbbed. Faint reddish marks glowed from his damp skin, as if his hand had been roughly twisted in a vise. "Some dream!" he thought.

Then the wolf walked in.

The monster stood at least three feet high at the shoulder, a great mass of muscle covered with thick, iridescent, gray fur. He strolled straight through our massive front door and into the center of our living room. On the canine's heels was a dapper young man, impeccably done up in a turn-of-the-century brown pinstripe suit, shiny black walking cane, and a fashionable derby perched on his slick brown hair. Turning toward Jack, his bony white lips curled into a menacing smirk.

"So you think there's nothing wrong with this house?!"

The demonic wolf's eyes bored straight into Jack, daring him to take even one breath. Mustering his most threatening grimace, Jack took one brave, deliberate step toward the intruders. No doubt the wolf would answer his bluff with a powerful leap, slamming Jack down to the floor while the snide man slid his long, spectral fingers around Jack's neck...

To his astonishment, the pair promptly vanished. Almost. The man's seething grin still pierced the musty air; the wolf's alabaster eyes gleamed faintly, straining to leave a final scar of doubt on Jack's waning bravado. Without waiting for an encore, Jack bolted straight into the kitchen for a calming glass of water...or possibly something stronger.

As Jack, trembling, reached for a glass, four-year-old Elise innocently toddled down the stairs and wandered up to her pale-faced father.

"What's the matter, Daddy? Did you see another one of our ghosts?"

one

How to Become a Ghost Magnet

*Vivian, do you know if anyone in
your family is a Sensitive?*

The question haunted me. Me, a Sensitive? Since the
day I took my first breath, my mother had filled me
with true tales of her family's precognitive Scottish second sight. The most famous tale began in the late nine-
teenth century in Glasgow, Scotland...

*Gray early-morning mist, too thick for even the gol-
den Scottish sunrise to penetrate, wound around a*

mud-spattered horse carting his daily wagonload of eggs and milk. A chilling air of desolation held the dawn captive as Janet Rattray Thompson, crying and panicked, raced down the narrow streets of Rutherglen. Her thick brown hair flew behind her in matted, wet curls; she pulled her rough woolen shawl close as she silently begged the rain to hold back just a few minutes longer. In response to her pleas, the pregnant clouds burst open upon her, sending buckets of rain streaming down the back of her dress and stinging her sky-blue eyes. Janet tripped in the deluge and landed on her knees in the middle of a mud puddle in the cobblestones. The streets seemed abandoned by all except for Janet, the milkman's wet nag, and a flock of black rooks who cawed mockingly at her. Janet crawled to her feet, hiked up her muddy skirt, and ran on. She took no notice that the wind had ripped the bonnet from her neck a mile ago. She had to reach William Dennie before he left for work. Before he died.

It was 1893, the year she was to marry her beloved Will. They had met only last year, introduced by Janet's uncles, who worked with William as analytical chemists at the Royal Gunpowder Factory. From the moment twenty-two-year-old Janet and William first smiled hello, they were inseparable. With eyes sparkling, they had spoken to the local minister, who couldn't resist giving them his heartiest blessings. Their highly anticipated wedding was to be six short weeks from now ... but only if William stayed home today.

William's front door finally materialized out of the fog. Janet flew at it and pounded as if to shatter every one of its massive oak boards. "God in heaven, let William be here. Don't let him leave for work. Not before I've spoken with him. Not ever."

The door creaked open and William peered out. One glance at his fiancé's tear-streaked face stopped his next breath. "Janet, dearest! What in God's name are ye doin' here, love? What's the matter?"

"William! William! Thanks be that you're still home!" she cried, falling into his arms and winding herself protectively into his gray woolen overcoat. "I'm so glad I'm in time!"

"Calm down an' tell me what's happened. Please, Janet—I'll be late for work now."

Five-foot-tall Janet became a blazing mountain of fire. She shoved her beloved back into his house and slammed the door soundly behind them. "Ye can not go to the factory this day!"

"What? Are ye daft?"

"I've had a dream, William! A terrible, horrible dream sent from God Himself. I saw ye dead! The factory blew up in a fire and ye were killed. It was so real, Will, so real. Stay home today! Maybe tomorrow, too. Just don't go in that laboratory today."

William laughed and crushed his beloved to his heart. "Janet, darlin', do ye fancy yourself a seer? I'm most frightfully sad that a nightmare scared ye, but what am I to say to your uncles as to why I didn't come in to work? 'I stayed home because Janet dreamed I should?' And what'll they think of me then? Dearest, if ye have some truth as to why the laboratory is in danger, then I'll listen, otherwise I have to leave. I'm a man of science, darlin', not dreams."

"William, it wasn't just a dream!" Janet clutched his arms. "It was more than that—more real. I saw ye killed in an explosion at the factory! It's a warning! A dire warning not to be taken lightly. Ye know that I foretell letters that will come in the next day's mail, and those same letters always come, even from friends not heard of for years. Will, please heed my dream and stay home today!"

With an amused smile, William planted a firm, quick kiss on his sobbing fiancé's lips. "Take care, sweet lass. I promise I'll come home safe to ye after work. Now I must go. Goodbye, m'love."

Three years later, Janet married William—but this William's last name was Hosie, not Dennie. Only a few hours after Janet's warning, chemical analyst William Dennie was killed in a freak chemical explosion at the Royal Gunpowder Factory. Part of Janet's heart died with him.

Janet Rattray Thompson Hosie was my great-grandmother.

Scottish second sight. Could such a thing be inherited, like eye color or medical traits? My mother swore that she didn't possess one speck of it herself, but she firmly believed in the talent, since she had witnessed her own mother's startling predictions. Mary Hosie strongly inherited her mother Janet's second sight. Like Janet and many other "gifted" women in our Scottish line, my grandmother Mary considered her unique talent as a gift from God that was to be taken seriously, but never, ever, flaunted as "predicting the future," which might smack of Occultism.

The Hosies were conservative, God-fearing Presbyterians who would literally cut off a hand before touching a tarot card. They insisted that they were nothing more than everyday women whose everyday lives were occasionally interrupted by dreams that came true.

Grandma Mary always kept her visions to herself, unless she felt that someone was in danger. Skeptics or not, the entire family took serious notice whenever Mary would quietly announce, "I've had a dream." Her most famous prophecy involved her younger sister, Agnes. For several nights in a row, Mary dreamed that the baby Agnes was carrying was born deformed and unusually small, almost shriveled. Frantic, she wired her sister, asking if everything was all right.

"Mary, the baby is developing just fine!" Agnes assured her. "The doctor has been keeping close watch and everything is perfectly normal."

My grandmother's horrific dream persisted. In June 1934, Agnes gave birth to Margaret Janet Jackson, a perfectly normal, healthy baby girl. Even so, Mary's nightmares of a shriveled baby persisted. Only a few days after her birth, newborn Margaret Janet was accidently dropped on her head by a butterfingered nurse, and the poor little girl's brain was irrevocably damaged. Margaret Janet died of cerebral palsy one month after her fourth birthday. She was always angelically beautiful, happy, bedridden, severely mentally disabled, and she never grew any larger than the size of a six-month-old baby…just as Mary had dreamed.

I can't predict letters in the mail, like my great-grandmother Janet Thompson, but sometimes I can tell who is calling me on the phone, even before it rings. And I've never predicted the future, although I've had a few dreams come true (it was nothing as dire as my grandmother Mary's dreams). Nope, I just see spirits everywhere I go. There isn't any mention of ghosts in my Scottish family's psychic history, so I seem to be the lone member plagued with the frustrating "gift" of sensing spirits, whether I want to or not.

Maybe I would have been spared paranormal worries during my early childhood had I not begun my life in a haunted house in Orlando, Florida, which just happens to be the same house where I now live and raise my children…but more about that later. My initial childhood fears were somewhat allayed by my mother's assurance that my eyes were just playing tricks on me. Mama was a staunch believer in Scottish second sight, but ghosts were another thing altogether. Even as a kid, I wasn't entirely convinced that she was right—but at least she never told me I was nuts. While she didn't discount special abilities, she didn't want to encourage me either, so my stories were brushed off as just that: stories.

That is, until we moved to our second house …

two

Spook Central

Lookout Mountain, Tennessee:
1970–1979

M ama? Mama? What *is* that?"
"Shhh! Be quiet!"

The footsteps had materialized at the bottom of the staircase, but where they had walked before that moment was a mystery. Dust paved the path up each step and down the long, ancient hallway toward the bedroom we occupied.

BAM!

BAM!

BAM!

Century-old plaster and floorboards shook with terror as each labored footfall met a stair. The sound sparked visions of a massive intruder in my fertile young mind, his shoulder blades sagging and screaming under the weight of the wretched, wasted life he bore for eternity. Any hope of spiritual redemption had vanished ages ago with his final living breath; all he had left was this house.

BAM!

BAM!

There were fifteen steps up the first flight of stairs alone, and each step he took required the energy of another lifetime.

Or, perhaps it was the house itself making all that noise?

BAM!

My mother and I lay petrified with fear in the center of the king-sized bed. Only two nights had passed since we first walked into this mammoth stone edifice that was to be our new home. It wasn't our choice; this was the only house we could afford to rent. My father never questioned why the grand old mansion hadn't kept a tenant in more than two years, especially at the dirt-cheap rate at which it was offered. The logical fact was that the house was in a bit of disrepair, but it was nothing that a few well-spent weekends with a hammer couldn't set straight. After all, it was the fifth house to ever be built on Lookout Mountain, and few buildings lasted sixty-five years without suffering a few creaky boards and loose wires.

Local legend insisted that the original builder was a member of the gentry who "died in his cups," which was an old Southern way of saying that he drank himself to death. The mansion was made of the same stuff as the ancient mountain on which it stood: layer after layer of chiseled brown stone, neatly stacked three stories high, surrounded on three sides by a massive stone-pillared veranda. The front walkway marched straight through a thick garden of buttery jonquils and under an ancient red and green maple tree that spanned the entire front of the house. One hundred ten years ago the ground had been soaked with Civil War blood. Eight cement steps, each one easily five feet long or more, connected the front walk to the porch, and the porch led to the front door.

On days when the clouds came down and covered the mountain, you could stand at the open front door and watch the gray blanket of pea-soup fog slide down our flowered walkway, up the eight front steps, and slither straight into the heart of the house. Like the wraith of the eruption of Mount Vesuvius, the ashen fog would cover everything, turning gardens to gloom, the red roofs to slate, and the sun to dusk. Anything farther away than your hand evaporated into the endless mass of mist. The fog haunted the mountain, and the mountain *became* the fog.

The front door opened into a room so large that it could have held King Arthur's Round Table, and I thought at one time it probably did. Row upon row of great rectangular windows stretched from ceiling to floor but shed little light on the shadows. Four men could easily have stood shoulder to shoulder inside the colossal stone fireplace that flanked the left wall. Double sets of pocket doors transformed solid walls into open archways, all of which led into a twisted labyrinth of eighteen rooms, three halls, two stairways, and the spookiest basement and attic this side of Dracula's dungeon.

I met the house on a snow-sifted night when I was nine years old. My parents and I had just driven ten straight hours from Orlando, Florida, to this Tennessee/Georgia border town, swapping our tropical palm trees and trade winds for a mile-high haunted mountain. My father had been accepted as the dean of students at the local college, which was located in a former turn-of-the-century luxury hotel that was almost as spooky as our house. Daddy's Midwestern no-nonsense logic left no room for ghost stories; he was simply happy to have a good job and a sturdy home.

The mountain mists had melded with the snowflakes as our little yellow Toyota Celica slid up the long, antiquated frozen driveway, which had originally been built for horse-drawn carriages. Moonlight bathed every ice crystal and turned the murky night into a sparkling Wonderland. I was elated. In my nine short years of life, the closest I had ever come to throwing a real snowball was kicking up beach sand on New Year's Day. I dashed out of the cramped car and started rolling in snow drifts that I imagined were deeper than the Grand Canyon. My Minnesota dad didn't have the heart to tell me this was only a half-inch flurry, so he joined my frozen romp. I loved it.

"Where's our house?" My blue Keds were soon soaked with cold and my toes ached for a hot bath.

Daddy pointed over my left shoulder. "It's right in back of you!" I turned and looked up … and up … and up. Stone by craggy stone began to emerge as the giant house materialized out of the night and loomed over me like the devil from Bald Mountain.

"It's going to eat us!" I gulped.

Two nights later, my prediction seemed to be coming true.

BAM!

BAM!

BAM!

"Did Daddy come back early from his trip?" I whispered to my mother as I lay stiff with terror beside her. Tonight was supposed to have been a Special Night: whenever my father was away on business, I was allowed the coveted childhood privilege of cuddling up next to Mama in the big bed. We would lay awake all night whispering stories and secrets that only mothers and daughters could share. No dark things that lived under the bed or in the back of the closet could touch me when I slept next to my mom...until tonight.

"Viv, even if he had come home, *that's not Daddy!*"

BAM!

The footsteps had climbed the main staircase and stopped on the landing that divided the ground floor from the second, which was one set of short stairs and half a hallway away from us. Why had the footsteps paused? Whatever it was wasn't gone. We could feel it waiting. Silence covered the house and stole our breath.

BAM!

It was climbing the second set of stairs that led to our hallway.

BAM!

That was two steps. How many steps were on that stairway? It was shorter than the first one...

BAM!

BAM!

BAM!

Silence. It had reached the top step and stopped again. We could feel it listening. My panicked mind raced over the second floor labyrinth: along each wall of the main, straight hallway stood rows of doors that opened into bedrooms and bathrooms and closets, all of which opened into each other and sometimes led into other smaller hallways. The bedroom in which my mother and I lay was located in the middle of the main hallway and was surrounded by doors that led to everywhere except out of the house. The only escape was either to walk down the haunted stairway and out the front door, or jump out a second-story window.

I stared at our closed bedroom door. "Mama, is it locked?"

My mother sat upright in the middle of the bed and shrugged in complete confusion. Her Presbyterian logic was still trying to reconcile what her ears heard. Fight took over my fright. Before I knew what I was doing, I jumped out of bed, made a beeline to the door, and snapped down the solid dead bolt. The click reverberated through the empty halls and rooms like a fog horn. I leaned my ear against the door and prayed like never before.

The doorknob in the adjacent bathroom began to rattle. My eyes met my mother's—was *that* door locked? No. Why would we have locked a bathroom door when we were the only two people in the house? I didn't dare risk leaving my guard post by our bedroom door to check the bathroom lock. This was all too little, too late, anyway; whatever was shaking that doorknob was closing in.

The rattling stopped, followed by a soft click. More silence. I swear, not even the clock ticked. Dead quiet. We turned our eyes toward the back of our bedroom, to the doorway that led into the closet, and then the unlit bathroom.

BAM!

BAM! BAM! BAM!

The footsteps had bypassed the bathroom door and boomed straight down the hallway toward our bedroom. I grabbed the glass doorknob in a death grip and leaned all seventy pounds of my weight against the door. There was no way I was going to let that grizzled, ghostly hand shatter the door and grab me by the—

Silence. Whatever was in the hall was standing on the other side of the door. Inches of wood separated us. The door and my lungs were ice.

Tap-tap.

I jumped back a foot. Something was feeling, searching around and over our door.

Tap-tap-tap-tap-tap.

Tap.

BOOM!

I would swear that our bedroom door visibly bulged and strained with every crashing pound. Terrified, I rushed back to the door and threw myself against it, praying that I could hold it closed.

"Vivian! Get away from there!" Mama cried from the bed.

Silence.

I was terrified beyond my worst nightmare. My entire body was shaking so hard that I was certain I was rattling the door more than the pounding intruder. I stared helplessly at my mom. How much more of this crazy cat-and-mouse game were we supposed to endure? This place would scare a skeleton to death! Mama's face was stark white. I wanted to protect her; I needed to protect her, but what more could I do? Pray. Just pray. I dutifully closed my eyes: "Dear heavenly father ..."

BAM!

BAM!

BAM!

The footsteps were moving away from our door. Slowly, deliberately, they thundered like cast-iron cannonballs down the remainder of the corridor and stomped into the empty front bedroom at the end of the hall.

It's checking out every room, I realized. *It knows we're here. It was trying to flush us out!*

The footsteps paused in the center of the empty bedroom, a few feet away from the door of a small, two-way closet that also opened into our room. The door on our side of the shared closet was shut tight; the door on the other side was shut tight. But neither door had a lock. I wondered how heavy the nearby dresser was and how fast an adrenaline-riddled kid could shove it in front of a closet door. The problem was that my skinny little legs were too frightened to move from where I stood against the bedroom door, and my terrified mother had yet to budge from the middle of the bed.

The quiet continued.

The intruder—a former resident?—remained in the next room, listening, staring, considering that connecting closet door. Once, I saw the door move—or was it just my strained vision? My mom always insisted that my eyes "played tricks on me" whenever I reported phantoms. I'll bet she was eating her words now.

BAM!

It was in the hallway again.

BAM!

BAM!

It was in front of our bedroom door.

Silence.

It was still in front of our bedroom door.

WHAM! WHAM! **WHAM!**

This time, we were certain that the century-old wooden door could not survive the ballistic pounding that slammed against it like a rabid rhino, again and again and again. Whatever wanted to get into our room, or force us out, was having one heck of a temper tantrum. I remained frozen to my self-ordered post, inches away from the shaking door, desperate to dive back into the center of the bed and my mother's arms but equally frightened of what would happen if the door did break and no one was ready to fight the intruder. I reached for the only nearby weapon: my hairbrush. I had no idea what I was going to do with it, but I at least I had something, and something was better than nothing.

Footsteps moved slowly down the hall. One. By. One.

BAM!

BAM!

BAM!

Silence. It was standing in front of the bathroom door again.

Silence.

Silence.

BAM!

It had reached the top step of the stairway.

Silence. Why on earth did those footsteps stop in front of every single door? Was it so old that it had forgotten that it had already investigated each room? Were each of its plodding footfalls as heavy as they sounded, so it needed to rest between each destination? Was this ghost burdened with chains, like Jacob Marley in *The Christmas Carol?*

No, I decided. It was a patient, hungry shark.

BAM!

BAM!

BAM!

BAM!

BAM!

Five steps down to the middle landing. Two minutes of insane silence.

BAM! BAM! BAM!

The ground floor reverberated. It had reached the bottom step of the main stairway. One more footstep and it would be on the ground floor, then into the living room. Our eardrums ached as we prepared ourselves for the next series of thunder stomps...but nothing happened. This time, the silence felt empty and exhausted, like the aftermath of a hurricane.

"Mama, is it gone?" I whispered as I finally crawled back in bed, still clutching my hairbrush.

"How could he be gone?" my mother replied through chattering teeth. "The footsteps stopped at the bottom of the stairs, but they haven't gone out the front door. He couldn't just evaporate!"

We listened to the tense, noiseless air. The house was quiet, but not calm. It, too, was listening for footsteps that never came. Everything was caught in the eternity between midnight and dawn…

Blistering sunshine pierced my sleeping eyelids. I moaned and pulled the blanket over my aching head. When were those stupid window curtains going to arrive from Sears? We never should have moved into a house without shades. I peeked one eye out from the covers, prairie-dog-style: according to my small, Big Ben alarm clock, it was well after noon! Mama *never* let me sleep this late! Faraway clinks and clanks of dishes being washed in the downstairs kitchen sink drifted under the bedroom door.

The door! I leaped out of my parents' big bed and inspected the closed entrance to the room: it was as solid as the wall. Every board was intact, not a single scratch or clawed-off piece of paint. Slowly I turned the glass doorknob and pushed outward, certain that I would find long, jagged fingernail lines etched deep into the opposite side of the door. The frame was unmarked on both sides. Maybe my ears had joined my eyes in playing tricks on me last night?

Should I tell Mama about my ghoulish nightmare? Probably not. My paranormal tales always ended up scaring her twice as badly as me, which then resulted in my being banned from watching *Dark Shadows* for yet another week. Barefoot, I plodded step by step, down one short, wooden stairway, past the spacious landing, down the second stairway, then rounded the corner onto the red brick floor of the kitchen. Stomp, stomp, stomp. I was never light on my feet.

"Hi, Mama! What time did you get up?" I asked as I slid two pieces of cracked wheat bread into the toaster.

"I didn't sleep all night!" Mama exclaimed. "I couldn't believe that you were actually snoring at four a.m.!"

"Oh, sorry! I promise not to keep you awake again if you let me sleep with you again tonight," I wheedled. "Daddy won't be back for another week!"

My mother stared at me in abject horror. "Vivian, you weren't the thing keeping me awake. Don't you remember those horrible footsteps last night? They went on for over twenty minutes!"

My stomach somersaulted. Last night wasn't a dream! It had been as real as the brick floor that was freezing my bare feet. My mother sat down at the table. She looked like she was about to vomit.

"Vivian, I have never, ever, in my whole life, been more scared than I was this morning when I had to walk down those stairs alone. I lay in bed for hours, waiting for you to wake up, but you never did and I didn't have the heart to disturb you. If *I* had been able to get to sleep after all that we went through last night, I don't think I'd want to ever wake up again!"

"Mama! You should have woken me up!" I wailed. From the time that I was a very small child, I was the self-proclaimed protector of my beloved mother. If she had a headache, I smoothed cool rubbing alcohol on her forehead; if she lay down for an afternoon nap, I guarded her door to make sure she was undisturbed; and if a midnight stomping ghost pounded on her door, I armed myself with a hairbrush.

Mama continued: "It was after ten thirty when I finally made myself crawl out of that bed. I got dressed, brushed my teeth, and did everything I could to avoid having to open that bedroom door. The upstairs hallway is always dark, but I swear it was beyond black when I stepped out into it this morning. I felt my way to the stairs and tiptoed down, certain that some lunatic was going to jump out of the woodwork and attack me." She looked nervously at me and my wide eyes. "Thank the Good Lord, no one else was in the house. I checked every nook and cranny, Viv. But, here's the strangest part of all: every single window and door was locked and dead bolted from the inside, just as I had left them last night!"

Mama took a deep breath. "Do you remember my telling you that half of the entire second floor of this house is divided off into a separate apartment? Our family has the entire ground floor and half of the rooms on the second floor, but the remaining rooms make up that apartment."

"Yeah," I replied. "You can only get into that apartment by walking up that rickety staircase that winds up the outside of the house from the driveway, straight up to the second floor. The guy who lives there is named Blair, right? He's got that big, bushy brown beard." Blair looked like Grizzly Adams but was as tame as a teddy bear.

"That's right, but there's also a door inside the house that connects Blair's apartment's kitchen to our second-floor hallway."

This was news to me. We had only moved in two days ago and my unpacking duties had left me little time to do a proper job of snooping around the twisted old mansion.

Mama continued her explanation: "Like most normal houses, the second floor was originally all part of one household. As decades went by, the owners decided to make a separate apartment out of part of the second floor, so they could have two families rent the house instead of just one, and get more money every month. There's a lock on each side of the door that's in between our two upstairs hallways. Does that make sense?"

"Yeah," I lied, making a mental note to investigate this mystery as soon as I had finished today's task of unpacking the rest of my books and toy box.

"Well," Mama continued, "I felt like an idiot, but I knocked on Blair's door this morning and told him all about last night's weird footsteps, then I asked if he had anyone staying with him. I was hoping that perhaps a confused guest had gotten up in the middle of the night, and had gotten lost in the dark trying to find the bathroom, and maybe ended up going through that connecting doorway that lead into our hallway."

"But, Mama!" I insisted, "Didn't you just say that our side of the connecting upstairs door is locked? Even if it wasn't, you know those footsteps started at the bottom of our stairs and disappeared when they went back down again. You said so yourself!"

"I know," my mother sighed, "but, I wasn't sure if that door was locked or not, and I was frantic for a logical explanation. It doesn't matter either way."

"Why not?"

Mama rubbed her pounding forehead. "Because, not only did Blair not have a houseguest, he wasn't even at home last night. Vivian, you and I were the only people in this entire building all night!"

I walked over to the cupboard, opened the utensil drawer, and pulled out our foot-long butcher knife. "I'm sleeping with *this* under my pillow tonight!" I announced.

My mother had been scared, but now she looked horrified. "You most certainly are *not*, especially if you intend to sleep with me again! You'll hear a bump in the night and slit my throat!"

Unknown to Mama, I made sure the knife was tucked under my pillow as I crawled into our shared bed that evening; surely Sir Galahad would have understood and applauded my heroic effort. My mother needn't have worried about my chaotic cutlass skills, because all that night, neither of us dared to close one eye, much less turn off the light, until the sunrise soothed us to sleep. The unexplained booming footsteps never returned, but they were just the drum major in the paranormal parade of things to come.

In spite of the ghostly footsteps, I claimed the large, empty bedroom at the end of the hall as my personal abode. It spanned almost a third of the entire second floor, with huge bay windows that offered a panoramic bird's-eye-view of the entire Chattanooga Valley stretched below our mountain. On winter nights, the mammoth maple tree in our front yard stood naked of leaves; its branches frozen into a silvery-white skeleton against the cold, black sky, while the lights of Chattanooga, located a mile below my window, sparkled up at me in rainbows of twinkling colors that would make the brightest galaxies jealous. During spring and summer, the tree re-dressed itself in a bright green blanket of star-shaped leaves that stretched over our roof and shielded my room from the blazing Tennessee sun. The fresh mountain breeze would swoop through my open shutters and frolic around my huge, haunted room, sending even the crankiest wraiths into a Maypole dance. The ancient tree was magical year-round, but it was nothing short of magnificent in autumn, when Jack Frost's first whisper sent the tree into enamored blushes of gold, crimson, chocolate brown, orange, and umber. The brilliance glowed like a fallen, burning star; it was the Fiery Diamond of Lookout Mountain.

"I live in a tree house!" It was the one truth I knew every time I looked out of my enchanted bedroom window, even decades later in my memory.

The fairyland that existed outside my bedroom windows evaporated when compared to the atmosphere that lurked inside my room. Although our entire house reeked of paranormal chaos, my bedroom in particular had earned the undisputed title of "the most haunted room in the house"—which was quite an achievement, given the spooky building's history. To describe the year-round temperature in my room simply as *cold* would be like calling the Abominable Snowman a snowflake: you could see your breath mist as you crossed the threshold of my doorway. While this paranormal air conditioning was welcomed at high noon in the middle of July, it was a different matter in the heart of a January ice storm. The old house had never had central air conditioning and the original 1905 heating system was never replaced or even updated, so all the rooms sported seventy-year-old free-standing, cast-iron radiators from which scalding steam would boil and hot water spurt. The only hope of warmth in my room in winter was to stand near enough to risk being scalded. I kept the radiator turned on in my room year-round, if only to thumb my nose at the frosty ectoplasm. I slept in a refrigerator, but it was worth it for the view.

One icy night, as I stood inches in front of my spurting and gurgling radiator, I felt long, thin fingers curl around my right shoulder blade and poke into my armpit. I was sure something that would have made even a banshee scream was looming behind me. Normal people would have fainted, but I was too startled at being touched to do anything except spin around and claw like a rabid tiger at the empty air in back of me. The feeling of the hand evaporated as the room fogged with frozen breath from my fast-moving lungs. The memory of that icy hand has stayed with me forever.

But my haunted room's Arctic climate was only icing on the paranormal pound cake: my great-grandmother's hyperactive rocking chair would merrily swing back and forth by itself while a decorative mobile that hung down from the ceiling would spin like a whirling dervish ... but only when my windows were shut tight. All of these nuisances paled in comparison to the problems my bedroom door gave me: not only did it swing wide open by itself, but as an added thrill, the doorknob would twist and unlock, as well! The favorite time for this antic was usually after I had crawled in bed and zipped myself up soundly inside my down-feather "mummy" outdoor sleeping bag, which was the only covering that kept me warm all night in the chilly room. Since I never turned my ceiling light off, I would pull the sleeping bag tight over my face and tie it shut with only my frozen, red nose sticking out for air. A few moments later, I would hear the distinctive squeak and click of my doorknob turning, followed by the rusty complaints of the door hinges. That darn door would swing open every night without fail the minute I tucked myself into bed for the night, no matter if it was ten p.m. or three a.m. Worst of all, the door slowly swung open to reveal the thick, inky blackness that filled the hallway and waited for me to join it.

The first time I poked my head out from my sleeping bag and actually saw the knob turn by itself, I jumped out of bed with my warm sleeping bag still zipped up to my waist, hopped awkwardly across the room, slammed the door shut, and shoved my heavy six-drawer dresser in front of it. The knob still stubbornly rattled from time to time, but my dresser didn't budge. After a few years, I got tired of dragging my furniture back and forth across my room each night, so I demanded that a dead bolt be placed on my door. My cynical father laughed at my request, but my best friend, who had his own experiences in our haunted house, promptly drove over with his electric drill. From that day on, my door never opened by itself again…but my doorknob still rattled.

It stood about knee-sock high, stretched as long as a skateboard, and was made of one solid block of coffee-colored wood that had been hand carved—or hacked—into some sort of squashed stool or table. Whatever it was, it had a head on it.

"What is it?"

My father grinned at me.

"This is a real witch doctor's stool from Africa!"

I stared at the hideous object. The rough sides had been coarsely axed into two Xs that served as short, solid legs for the chair, with rows of lines and dots and zig zags and Xs carefully painted with a thin, black liquid that resembled ink. These marks weren't decorations; every symbol had a meaning, unknown to all but the African priest who made it. The top (or back) of the bench had been smoothly carved into a flat seat that was more long than wide and was polished to a high gloss, probably from years of use by the witch doctor who sat on it.

The head was worst of all. It jutted out on a "neck" from the front of the polished seat, like a turtle yanked out of its shell. It had two painted black "eyes," a slit that resembled a mouth, and was shaped like a rotten pear.

"It's for you, Viv!"

What kind of a person would give a nine-year-old kid an actual witch doctor stool? Genuine sacred artifacts are rarely passed around, much less one that had as many scary vibes as I felt from this one. Perverse child that I was, I was captivated.

"It's from old Auntie Grace." My dad answered my question before I had time to ask it. "Do you remember her? She's one of Granddaddy's missionary friends. She's been working in Africa and made friends with the priest of a local tribe. He gave her this stool, which he used to sit on when he would mix potions or heal people. She said it's a monkey fetish chair."

I stared at the little head, trying hard to convince myself it looked like a monkey instead of a sick turtle.

My dad chuckled at my confusion. "Monkey paws are used in some African religions to cast *juju* spells, so I guess that's why this stool is carved in the shape of a monkey. Auntie Grace thought this little stool would be the perfect size for you to use as a TV chair. Hey! You can sit on it while you watch *The Monkees!*"

I was young enough to think that my father's pun was hilarious.

"But, Daddy, did the witch doctor practice good magic or bad magic with this stool?"

"Well, he was a friend of Auntie Grace, so I'm sure that he was a good witch doctor." My father regarded the stool as nothing more than a piece of cultural furniture, so he was happy to attach any fairy tale to it that I liked.

As I dragged the small bench across the room and planted it four feet in front of our big Sylvania TV set, I overheard my mother's worried whisper:

"Phillip, do you really think this is an appropriate thing to give to a child? Vivian is right; we don't know exactly what this stool was used for. It looks creepy."

My father rolled his eyes. "Jeannie, it's just an old wooden chair from an African tribe."

I plopped myself on top of the stool's smooth seat, with my long, skinny legs squatted out like a bullfrog. It was pretty comfortable for a hunk of rock solid wood. I ran my hand across the top of the conical head in front of me. I felt nothing except cold, hard timber and...ouch! I wondered if the African priest had gotten splinters in his hand, too.

As was suggested by Auntie Grace, the stool became my TV buddy. Together we watched Saturday morning cartoons, an endless array of World War II movies with my veteran dad, and every episode of *The Sonny and Cher Comedy Hour.* The monkey was mesmerized.

My mom never breathed one word to me of her worries about the mysterious stool. Its reported magical history made her uncomfortable, and she didn't like the feeling she got when she was in the same room as it. She swore that it watched her with those black eyes. Still, mom kept her mouth shut. My cynical dad had never stopped teasing her for her "story" about those invisible giant foot stomps the night he was away.

Mama always insisted that she didn't inherit a speck of Scottish second sight, but three years later, her intuition about that spooky chair was proven right. I was now twelve years old and excited to finally be left alone in the house at night without a babysitter. The truth was that most of my sitters weren't keen on returning to our haunted house for more than one job—they were paid to watch a kid, not an array of ghosts.

"Are you sure you'll be all right, sweetheart?" Mama asked for the eighth time as my father dragged her out the front door.

"Jeannie, she'll be fine. We're only going out to dinner for a few hours."

I blew my parents a big kiss and happily shut the door behind them. Alone at last! This was my first big step toward being a grown up. Before long, I would have my own string of babysitting jobs—if I could just survive tonight in my haunted house.

I quickly realized freedom had a price. I was bored. Hmm. What to do? Daddy watched TV at night and Mama did the dishes. I opted for Daddy's plan and picked up my trusty monkey stool.

The smoky cloud appeared in front of my head like a rude puff from a giant cigar, then formed into—of all things—a large triangle that hovered and snapped at my face. I didn't know whether to be more terrified or confused. What the heck *was* it? Who ever heard of a floating, biting triangle? I tried to brush it away, but the obstinate thing kept slamming at me again and again. I felt like I was being attacked by the wraith of a billiard rack!

My arms began to ache. I glanced down. The inky black eyes of the wooden monkey head glared back.

After all these years, alone at last . . .

I found I was still gripping the *juju* stool! With a yelp, I dropped the chair like a ton of bricks, which is exactly what it felt like as it smashed on my feet. I glanced back up. The triangle was shooting straight at me for another hit.

I have no idea how I ended up in the bathroom, but I stayed behind that locked door until I heard my mother's frantic knock on the other side.

"Vivian! Vivian! Are you in there?"

If I was eleven, I would have thrown the door wide open and rushed into my mother's arms, sobbing, "MOM-MEEEE!" However, I was not eleven. I was *twelve*, and this was my first night left alone. I flushed the toilet.

"Mama! For gosh sakes, can I have one minute of privacy, please?"

My mother continued to shout through the shut door. "Vivian, why didn't you answer us? Didn't you hear us come in? We've been looking all over this house for you. We were scared out of our minds! And why are all the lights out? We thought you'd been kidnapped!"

The house was dark? Every lightbulb had been blazing during the triangle attack. I opened the door and strolled out of the bathroom like it was a red carpet.

"Mama, I'm perfectly fine. I think your eyes were just playing tricks on you."

No one ever asked why I moved the monkey stool permanently into the back of the hall closet, with the head carefully shoved into the corner like a disgraced imp. Sitting on special TV chairs was for little kids and witch doctors, anyway.

The noisy "wind" we called Joe Blow never allowed us a full night's rest. Windy nights on Lookout Mountain were sometimes equal to tropical storm–force gales in the rest of the world. The crazed wind would pelt down our brick chimneys and bellow like a wounded moose suffering from chronic indigestion. The sound brought to mind visions of Pepto Bismol and unclean bathrooms. The strange thing was that the fireplace in my parents' bedroom was not only the loudest but the *only* fireplace in the house that experienced this nightly gastronomic symphony. My dad could have slept through the next world war, but my poor mother hadn't trusted a single squeak since our terrified night with the stomping footsteps. Desperate for a good night's sleep, Mama finally duct taped a large metal sheet in front of their fireplace opening, with prayers that this would thwart the noisy wind. The result was an even more ghastly assortment of moans and groans and sounds of general flatulence. "Great," my mom sighed. "I've given the fireplace the farts."

Joe Blow was the ghost who wasn't a ghost. At least, that's what we told ourselves. But it wasn't just my room or my parents' fireplace that had otherworldly perks. Every spooky basement and haunted attic shown in every horror movie was probably modeled after the ones in our stone mansion. Those two areas were so creepy that they were irresistible to a precocious kid like me ...

"If I had a nice, big attic like this when I was a little girl, I would have made it my clubhouse and held secret meetings with all my friends!"

Mama was urging her nine-year-old daughter to take an attic that would send Dracula flapping away in fear and turn it into a fun play space. After moving in, we assumed the only entrance to the attic was through the full-length door that opened from Blair's kitchen in his second floor apartment ... until the day I inspected the short hallway that connected our living spaces and discovered a short door perched four feet above the floor! There were no steps or ladder leading to it; it was just a small Alice in Wonderland door suspended in the middle of the hidden hallway. Sarah Winchester, the haunted owner/architect of California's twisted Winchester Mystery House, would have loved it.

Hidden doors and passages in our house were as common as a winter cold; I only worried that my new discovery would open in to another boring, empty closet. Still, a new door is a new door, and an immediate investigation was launched. I dragged a chair to the base of the door, stood on the seat cushion, and strained my arm up toward the floating doorknob. I expected the usual short twist to a locked deadbolt, but to my amazement, the door swung easily open. Musty smells of cedar and dust wafted outward. I stuck my head into the dark passage, expecting to see closet shelves, but instead beheld a mammoth stairway! Why would a door in the middle of a tiny, hidden hallway open onto the middle of a big old flight of forgotten stairs? There were faint clinking sounds of glass and metal, as if pots and pans were being washed in a sink. I turned my head toward the sound and saw a thin line of light far below me at the bottom of the stairway. Could that be the door to Blair's kitchen?

I switched on my flashlight. Chocolate brown wooden stairs, as wide and stately as those on Scarlett O'Hara's forgotten plantation, emerged from the darkness. I pulled myself up through the suspended doorway, sat on the nearest step, and pointed the flashlight beam down toward my left. Sure enough, the stairway descended into the back of a closed door. I could see the open frame of the ancient skeleton key lock illuminated from the kitchen light that beamed out from the other side. Blair was doing his dishes, with no idea or care of his attic's invasion. He seldom bothered to open that door, anyway.

Satisfied, I turned my flashlight beam upward to the darkness on my right. Up, up, up, up…did these stairs ever end? There was no other option but to climb them and see what lay at the top.

Each step of the newfound staircase creaked and groaned, as all proper dark and mysterious passages should. I crept up slowly, unsure of what my foot might land on next. My head was beginning to pound from the dust-riddled air, but I didn't dare cough or sneeze. Suddenly, I felt the room open up around me, cold and damp, as if I had climbed up into a cave. I was in the middle of a vast, wooden triangle, the underbelly of the A-lined roof. I had found the attic. Tree-trunk thick beams of dark wood met at the highest point in the middle of the ceiling, then sloped down on either side until they touched the floor against the east and west walls. A grown man could stand up in the center of the attic, but nothing bigger than a dust bunny would fit in the cubby holes along the sides.

The room had no end. It began at the top of the hidden staircase and spanned the entire width of the second floor, but as far as my flashlight beam would shine, there was no rear wall to be seen. Was this place like C. S. Lewis's magical wardrobe to Narnia … except bad? Whatever dark thing lurked back there was not to be disturbed.

What *was* back there?

On the other hand, the front part of the spooky attic was filled with decades of wonder! A stack of sealed wooden boxes had been undisturbed since 1932, according to their labels. A lady's straw cloister hat lay next to a rusty exercise bicycle and a cracked plastic bedpan. Most important of all, there was a child's wooden play table and three chairs lodged in a corner a few yards from the top of the stairway. Surely this was a sign that this place was meant to be my clubhouse!

I discovered a hidden wall switch that activated a dusty, yellow light bulb dangling just in front of the entrance to the stairs. The back of the attic was still in shadows, but the front half of the attic blinked awake under the dim light. With a gulp, I offered a compromise to the dark thing in the back corner:

"I won't bother you back there if you don't bother me up here. Okay?"

I didn't hear a thing. A lack of reply was good enough to inspire me to brave the dark and get to work on my clubhouse. After getting the okay from Mama and neighbor Blair, I spent the rest of that week climbing up and down the hidden staircase, toting up drawing paper and crayons and toys and books and costumes and other clubhouse necessities. (I left the voodoo monkey stool downstairs.) The mysterious table and chairs, abandoned by long-ago children, was re-decorated with a layer of bright red paint and yellow happy face stickers. I covered the surrounding dusty attic beams with posters of kittens and rainbow-colored peace signs. The Lookout Mountain Kids Only Clubhouse was open for business! There was just one small problem: all of my friends were scared of the attic.

In the end, there were only two regular members of my club: me and the dark thing that always watched me from the back of the endless attic. Most of the time, it left me alone with my toys and goosebumps, but once in awhile, I swore that I could see the black shadow move a little closer to me…and a little closer…and even though it was still very far away, tucked back in the farthest shadows, I would beat a hasty retreat down the stairs. Especially when I heard growling!

The basement—or, as we more appropriately referred to it, the Dungeon—was an underground maze of two cavernous chambers and three smaller rooms, all twisted around the original, very dilapidated fifty-gallon hot water heater nicknamed the Monster. The criminally insane Monster lived in the center of the Dungeon and was responsible for supplying all of the hot water and steam heat to every bathroom, kitchen sink, and radiator in the house, including our neighbor Blair's apartment. Since the upstairs apartment had no direct access to the basement, it was the responsibility of the occupants of the main house (my family) to routinely check the Monster's finicky pressure. If the pressure wasn't checked, the Monster would—as Stephen King would use to great effect in *The Shining*, written that same decade—blow the house, humans, ghosts, and a good part of the surrounding neighborhood to the third moon of Pluto. Every five to seven hours, the blistering hot, cast-iron pressure valve had to be spun around and around in order to release a blast of scalding steam and bubbling water, which was the only remedy to return the explosive pressure gauge to normal. We turned it before we had brushed our teeth in the morning, we turned it after saying bedtime prayers, and we turned it in-between. If we left on vacation, we had to find a Monster sitter. Our next door neighbors knew how to turn that valve; my childhood friends knew how to work it; I think we were trying to teach Rufus the red setter that lived down the street how to do it, too. The constant threat of the finicky hot water heater blowing up was a looming apocalypse that worried everyone, including the ghosts.

The Dungeon had two entrances: the first was a short, steep, stone stairway that was located on the outside of the house and plunged straight down through nets of ancient cobwebs and mold into thick shadow. Hidden at the shadow's end was a plain, windowless door, which was always locked tight with a shiny brass padlock that had no key. Had anyone dared to break the cursed lock, the rusted door hinges would moan open to the gaping basement.

The second Dungeon door was located inside of the house, hidden on the far end of the tiny, dark breakfast nook that sported a ceiling so low that those entering through its narrow doorway had the urge to stoop down in order not to bump their heads. This was only an optical illusion, sort of like a scene out of Alice in

Wonderland's drunken nightmare. I often imagined that someone had laundered the breakfast nook in scalding water and shrunk it, while the rest of the building's ceilings remained so high that a small giraffe could stand up comfortably. It was my creative mother who had dubbed this small room off the kitchen the breakfast nook, but I gruesomely referred to it as the Embalming Chamber. Mama was determined to turn this shadowed space into a cozy cove: she painted the peeling walls glistening white and plastered bright orange flowered curtains in front of the row of small windows that provided a panoramic view of the eerie outside stone stairway that lead down to the basement. Nothing could conquer the room's gloom; even when all of the lights went out in the house, which often happened, this space was always darker. This particular infestation was probably due to the inky blackness that seeped in from beneath the basement door. Needless to say, we preferred to eat our meals in the dining room.

The interior basement door always opened with a spine-splitting CREEEEEAK! that would have made Vincent Price proud. A half-rotted, wooden stairway leading from the breakfast nook down to the basement floor hugged the right side of the chiseled stone wall; the opposite side was covered with rows and rows of sturdy, wooden shelves that could have held a restaurant's worth of canned foods. The problem was that as the stairs went down, the long pantry shelves remained at the same level, which meant the far end of the shelves was impossible to reach without balancing, tiptoed, on the edge of the creaking stairs.

A bare yellow light bulb just inside the doorway provided a dim glow down the stairs, but once your foot hit the basement floor, the only way to see was to feel your way through the cold blackness into the center of the main room just in front of the gurgling Monster, and then pull on a long string that hung down from a ceiling light bulb. The string was only two hops away from the bottom of the stairway, but those were the longest strides in the world, because on the other side of the Monster was a small stone alcove that was the spookiest place of all.

The shadowed hollow was almost invisible: a dirty, forgotten hole, where rusty water pipes twisted up through the floor and crashed into walls. It was the perfect spot for a murderer to hide a mutilated body— I could almost see rotted arms and legs stuck against the craggy stone walls. Whatever lurked back there had something dire to hide and would rather kill than confess. Every time I dared myself to step into the bowel of that black corner, I felt something evil loom up…and I would run away! This was separate from the other ambiguous things that roamed around the basement and peeked under the door. The thing in the dark alcove stayed there, and only there. Alone.

I was happy enough to avoid that dank little corner, but a girlish whim brought me face to face with my fear one summer night. I can't remember where I found the old book, or even what the title was, but it was filled with superstitions from the past that enthralled me as a teenager. One chapter promised that if a young woman wanted to know whom she would marry, she must walk slowly backward down unlit basement stairs at midnight, holding a lighted, white candle in her left hand and a mirror in her right, which was to be held over her left shoulder. When the woman reached the bottom step, the face of her future husband would appear in the mirror…although the narrative neglected to explain how anyone would be able to see this image in the darkness. But logic is scarce and magic is queen when you're fourteen years old, so one warm night, after my mother was asleep and my dad was comfortably swaddled in his recliner and mesmerized by the late, late movie on TV, I dug my great-grandmother's ivory hand mirror out of our hope chest and opened the basement door.

A blast of frigid air, colder than the usual iciness that slithered through the basement, smacked my face so hard that I caught my breath…and I hadn't even placed my foot on the top stair yet! I peered down the gaping stairway, past the endless sentry shelves stocked with canned soups and deviled ham. It seemed as if the basement's blackness had gathered in one large mass at the base of the stairs, fifteen steps below where I stood in the flickering light of my white candle. Something was waiting for me, daring my teenage stupidity to continue the dubious little psuedo-spell.

What the heck am I doing? I paused to consider some possible consequences. It was way too easy to fall down these rickety stairs with all the lights on, much less walking backward in the dark when I was half-asleep! What if I dropped my candle and set the house on fire? What if I tripped and broke my neck and joined the basement wraiths? *Nah. That will never happen to me. I'm too young to die.*

Armed with the youthful myth of immortality, I turned my back to the basement, placed my left heel on the top wooden step, and took one blind step backward toward the phantoms. Candlelight flickered in my left hand as I obediently stared into the dark reflected in the mirror.

Second step.

Creak.

Was that my foot?

Third stair.

Fourth.

Keep breathing.

Five. Six. Seven.

Take it slow.

Eight.

Wish there was a handrail.

Nine ...

What's on my back?!

A blast of cold vomited up from below, sliced into my spine, and froze my body, despite the scalding steam that sputtered from the cast-iron intestines of the Monster not far away.

Hands. I could feel something cold, cold, pushing against my back. Not hands. Just pressure...right? My body turned into a tangle of needles. My lungs shrank; I could see my gasps form clouds through the candle-light. Too terrified to turn around and face my fear, my eyes crawled to the mirror's glass that I still clenched like death in my right fist over my shaking left shoulder. Was there a face?

I tore up the stairs, slammed the door shut, hit the deadbolt twice, backed up against the opposite wall, and stood frozen, staring at the blackness pulsing under the door. My candle had gone out, but Great-Grandma's magic mirror was still in one piece. Something was scratching, very softly, on the basement side of the locked door. *It was probably mice*, I assured myself. *Or rats.*

There was no doubt in my mind after that day that the basement was haunted. No one ever argued that fact, although few would audibly admit it. The main room, home to the Monster, opened onto another large room that contained nothing except a mountain of forgotten coal piled in a far corner and an axe. The only escape from this area of the basement was through the padlocked door that had no key. On the far side of the axe room stood a narrow doorway that lead to Shangri-La: a cozy little workroom with bright electric light and walls of shelves stuffed with the discarded belongings of every handyman since the house was built. The Good Hardware Fairy must have blessed this small space because, in addition to being the only room in the basement that was not haunted, for some reason, the phantoms never dared cross its threshold. It felt protected. If I could make it past the Monster and the dark alcove, then I was safe as long as I remained in the little workroom with the bright light on. The light was very important. I loved the enchanted little workroom and spent many hours, long into the night, working on projects made of wood and leather and paint, while frustrated wraiths watched me from the other side of the open doorway. Problems only arose when I inevitably had to turn out the light and race back through the dark with the devil on my back. Considering my cold bedroom and the prospect of running past the Monster late at night, I really should have just moved a bed into that workroom.

If twenty-eight-year-old Blair had lived in Minnesota, he would have been Paul Bunyan. His bushy brown beard was as wide as his locomotive shoulders and as large as his Adam's apple. One glance at his six-five frame clomping down a forgotten mountain trail sent the biggest black bears into early hibernation. No one messed with Blair...and Blair messed with no one. He was as gentle as cotton candy, and Wendy loved him.

Although they had been engaged for over a year, Wendy seldom stepped into Blair's apartment and made every excuse possible to continue her absence. His place was just plain spooky. She had already postponed their wedding date twice because Blair said that he couldn't afford anywhere else for them to live except his spooky apartment. Wendy wasn't superstitious, and she certainly didn't believe in ghosts; she just felt as if the apartment didn't want her there, and she wasn't sure that it liked Blair, either.

"I know this sounds crazy," she would admit to my sympathetic mother, "but, I swear when I'm alone in Blair's kitchen, I can hear footsteps walking up behind me! Not the big, stomping ones that you said that you heard on your side of the house; these are just the normal walking kind…but, they're solid footsteps and there is never anyone behind me when I turn around!"

Blair never disbelieved his fiancé's or my mother's spooky stories, but as long as his life was undisturbed, he didn't worry about it…until one horrific night.

He had gone to bed on this particular night giddy with joy: Wendy had finally agreed to a date for their wedding and promised to stick with it, no matter where they ended up living after the ceremony—as long as he promised to spend the next day looking at six other places to live. She had even stopped by his apartment to consider if there was enough space for her furniture to join his.

Blair had snuggled into his bed and fallen into the blissful sleep of an unburdened soul. Wendy was really going to marry him this time; no more excuses about spooky footsteps or feeling "watched" by something in the kitchen. He felt safe.

A soft growling noise rippled through the dark bedroom.

"Wendy?"

Blair's sleepy eyes popped open. There was someone standing in his dark bedroom with him. He glanced over at the illuminated digital clock.

"Hon, it's after two! What are you doing here? Turn on the light." Wendy had never walked into his apartment unannounced, especially in the middle of the night. Blair sat up in bed and leaned over to turn on the floor lamp. His hand froze before it reached the switch.

A brown mass, like a man-sized cloud, floated inches in front of his open bedroom doorway. Caught in moonlight from the bare window, parts of the foggy form glowed like the captain of the Flying Dutchman.

Oh, m'gosh! Blair thought to himself in terror, *the house is on fire!* He threw back his blanket to leap out of bed, but the dark mass suddenly moved toward him. This was no fire. There was no smell of smoke; just an overwhelming odor of excrement that made Blair's churning stomach swell up into his mouth.

There was no time for logical reasoning. In a blink, the brown fog-thing slid across the room, surrounded Blair's bed, and swallowed him whole. Blair swore that a rotten rubber noose had been knotted across his esophagus; every bit of air he inhaled burst from his mouth as a weight collapsed against his lungs. Whether he passed out or rolled out from under the attack on purpose, somehow Blair ended up on the floor beside his bed. Gasping, he raced toward the open doorway on his hands and knees and then struggled to his feet against the living room sofa. Behind him, the smoke monster swelled with disdain as it turned from the tangled bed and slid across the abandoned bedroom toward its escaped prey.

With a cry, Blair staggered through the dark living room, into the kitchen, and crashed against his locked front door. The murderous smog was already halfway across the sofa and would engulf him again in two gasps. Blair twisted the cold deadbolt. It wouldn't budge. He hit it again. The smoke monster was licking his shoulder.

Blair gathered his lumberjack bulk and smashed his entire 273 pounds against the petrified lock. The door smashed through its frame as Blair tumbled down two levels of outside stairs and landed in a heap on the gravel driveway. He would spend the next few nights in the hospital, and even more months after that limping around in a cast—but what was a broken foot or a cracked collar bone compared to saving your immortal soul?

"I think I need to go to church," Blair confided to Wendy, "and I don't mean just for our wedding ceremony!"

A few weeks after Blair vacated the apartment, a young college student and his dog moved in. We never told him the real reason why Blair had suddenly moved out after five years. We just blamed it on long-suffering Wendy.

I was eighteen years old on the last day that I ever set foot in our massive, magical, haunted Tennessee house. Finances, not ghosts, had forced us to move: during the decade that we had lived there, the greedy out-of-state owner—who had never set eyes on the magnificent stone building in his life—decided that it would be more profitable to tear down the old house and turn the property into a paid parking garage. The house stood a block from the Incline Railway and a short walk from Pointe Park and its gift shops—think of the hundreds of tourist dollars that could be gleaned from a conveniently located parking garage! When his renters refused to break their lease and leave of their own accord, he simply began to raise the monthly rent to astronomical amounts until our checkbook couldn't take any more. My father relocated us to a smaller, very cozy, very un-haunted house just a few miles away on the Georgia side of the mountain. We were sorry to leave our stone mansion; we had grown to love it, despite the ghosts.

I was the last person in my family to leave the house. The moving van had hauled away our belongings, we had swept away the last cobweb, and the old house, which had begun life eight decades before as royalty, once again stood alone, empty and lost under the maple trees. Its rooms would never ring again with my mother playing

"Clair de lune" on our antique piano. There would be no more birthday parties, no Christmas trees, no trick-or-treaters at Halloween. The next visitor would be a backhoe and a wrecking ball. Not even my magical maple tree would escape execution.

"I'm going back to check the house one more time," I shouted to my mother as the empty moving van pulled out of our new driveway. "I think we may have left one of our brooms there." My excuse was plausible and transparent. Not only did I miss our old house, but I felt that I needed to walk through it one final time. All by myself. I had grown up in that house and I needed to reach closure with the ghosts. The old house was only a couple of miles away, so I grabbed the car keys and drove toward Brow Road.

As I pulled into the driveway for the last time, my heart thumped in my throat as it had when I first saw the haunted house. Why did we love it so much? Had we not endured a myriad of ghostly shenanigans that would have made Stephen King catch his breath? This house had filled my innocent childhood with stalking monster footsteps, haunted bedrooms, doors that opened to wake me up, chairs that rocked themselves to sleep, unseen hands that grabbed me from behind, groans, moans, wraiths, wayward rats, and a hot water heater that was on the brink of creating the next Armageddon.

On the other hand, the Victorian stone mansion had shown me the splendor and grace of an era that was long gone even before my mother had been born. The house had raised me among magical pocket doors that disappeared into walls or created rooms within rooms; I was accustomed to coils of cast-iron radiators that spat like a disgruntled old woman but warmed you like a grandmother; I knew windows that touched the floor and ceiling, and a stone fireplace that was so big that I could stand upright in it. That fireplace was one of my best friends: it had given me golden memories of cold Halloween nights filled with popping corn and melting marshmallows as my friends and I crowded around the crackling fire in the dark living room and dared each other to quote haunted old poems that ended with "…and the goblins they'll GIT ya if ya DON'T WATCH OUT!"

I had learned to face my terrors, real or imagined, by walking backward down a dark basement stairway and building a clubhouse in the belly of the haunted attic…just not too near the back. My friends and I had dumped winters of melted snow from our frozen boots onto the hardwood floors, turned the stairway landing into a playroom, and transformed half of the living room into a theatre stage on which we performed everything from Beatles dance skits to a full-blown production of *Camelot*. The house had laughed with our endless parties and hidden Easter eggs that were found just before we ate our Thanksgiving turkey. This house was haunted with much more than just a few cranky ghosts—it was filled with love. It was an abused queen who had lived well past her prime but still had decades of charm and strength left in her. She did not deserve a death sentence.

I stood on the stone veranda for the last time. How many tea parties had we held on this porch? How many hours did I spend agonizing over afternoon math homework spread out all over the steps and chairs? I had entered this house as a child, and now I wandered through the front door for the last time as a young woman on the brink of adulthood. The silence hurt my ears.

"I'm here to say goodbye," I called out loud. My voice echoed through the empty, listening rooms. The house made no reply. I headed toward the basement door, tiptoed down the rickety staircase, and dumped the overflowing steam from the Monster one last time. The dark thing in the dark corner was still there, waiting. It would still be there when the unsuspecting college student, who refused to move out of Blair's haunted apartment, took over as caretaker of the furnace, and it would be there to greet the demolition crew.

"You know, they're going to tear this house down," I called out to the shadows. "I just wanted to let you know that."

As I walked up the basement stairs, I could feel the familiar movement behind me...but this time it followed me through the closed door and into the rest of the house. As I wandered from room to room, I swore I picked up one or two more unseen companions as I crossed each doorway. I had become a paranormal Pied Piper. Bright, afternoon sunlight streamed through every window. It was probably just my eyes playing tricks on me.

I reached the main interior stairway and paused. Something was waiting for me at the top. I could feel it. Even my unseen entourage drew back, unwilling to climb up with me. Fools rush in where angels—and Others—do not dare.

Step by step, I slowly climbed the staircase, just as the pounding phantom footfalls had done ten years earlier. Now it was my turn to inspect each room, one by one, to find out what was waiting inside. Sunlight continued to flood the house; the white tiles of each bathroom sparkled and sunbeams danced around every bedroom and trickled into the closets. Only the attic remained as dark and foreboding as ever, but I had decided that my self-imposed Personal Closure Ceremony required that I walk every step in that entire house from top to bottom. No matter what followed me. The yellow eyes blinked from the back shadows as I dusted off my little table and chairs.

It wasn't until I entered my second-floor bedroom that trouble began. I stood alone, gazing through my beloved picture windows and soaking in my final treetop view of the world when I heard the footsteps behind me. They were solid, and they meant business. It was time for me to leave, but I would never leave this house running scared, no matter what stepped on my frightened toes. Head held high like a proud soldier, I forced myself to walk slowly, step by step, out of my room and down the sunlit hallway. I paused deliberately in front of each room to make sure that every door was standing wide open and sunlight carpeted my final exit. After all the years of paranormal chaos that I had endured, I deserved some respect!

My ghostly escort's footfalls echoed every one of my own. It was on my heels, like a Nazi guard. My resolve finally crashed on the stairs: I reached the mid-stairway landing and bolted like the Mad March Hare down the rest of the steps, through the unseen assembly that still waited by the kitchen, made a beeline straight toward the front door ... and stopped, laughing. There, waiting for me just inside the doorway, stood the wayward broom that I had originally returned to retrieve!

BAM!

A door slammed from somewhere on the second floor. From the sound of it, I figured it was probably the bathroom.

BAM!

A second door swung shut. This came from my parents' room, which was the next one down the hall. The closet would be next.

The house echoed with the crash of each upstairs door shutting, one by one down the line. Was I being given a spectral twenty-one gun farewell salute, or a final warning to get out? I paused by the broom for an answer.

The footsteps started at the top of the stairway. Clomp. Clomp. Clomp.

Broom in hand, I jumped out onto the porch, shoved the key into the front door, and locked the house behind me. For good.

A few weeks after we moved out, the City of Lookout Mountain refused to legally allow the owner to demolish the building. Not only was it the fifth house built on the mountain and therefore a historic landmark, but more importantly, no one wanted an eyesore parking garage smack in the middle of one of their beautiful neighborhoods. To this day, on the edge of Lookout Mountain, across the street from the bluff and a block down from the Incline Railway, my haunted house still stands proudly in the same spot that it has stood for over a century. The magical maple tree is gone, the grape arbor has been cleared away, and the gravel carriage path has been transformed into a sensible circular brick driveway. But the ghosts are still there. I know, because every once in awhile, my memories melt into nightmares. Still, I wouldn't trade a single one. After all, how many kids get to grow up with ghosts?

three

Final Exams at the Riddle House

West Palm Beach, Florida:
1979-1980

Y ou know this house used to be a funeral parlor."
It was the vocal epitaph of the freshman girls' dorm.
"They displayed the dead bodies in the front window!"
"Oh, *shut up!*"

What person in their right mind would believe any-thing college guys had to say, especially to a gaggle of innocent teenage girls on their first day of university life? Like the rest of my freshman class, I had been yearning for this first official day of adult freedom for the past eighteen years of my life … but for a different reason than most kids. I didn't care about getting out on my own to see the big world—I just wanted to get away from the ghosts. Since the day I was born, I had ended up in one haunted house after another. We would drive from our haunted home in Tennessee to spend family vacations at my grandfather's paranormal palace in Orlando. Even Disney World had a Haunted Mansion! I spent every spare minute of my senior year of high school dissecting mountains of college pamphlets, all displaying photos of contemporary, ghost-free campuses. My mother wanted me to go to a Christian school and, besides escaping my paranormal housemates, I wanted a South Florida beach. Palm Beach Atlantic College was the answer.

The small campus was founded in 1968 by a group of citizens from Palm Beach County who wanted a Christian college in the area. By 1972, the fledgling school was accredited by the Southern Association of Colleges and Schools and proudly graduated its first senior class. Seven years later, I was accepted to join the suntanned student body, so I hopped a bus from Overlook Mountain, Georgia, to my grandfather's haunted house in Orlando … and was stranded. On the very day that PBA was to open for fall classes, just before Labor Day weekend, West Palm Beach was smacked by Hurricane David. Although the storm's winds actually fell just below official hurricane strength, it was enough to cause the intercostal waterway to flood, which closed the campus and delayed opening day for a week.

"I hope this isn't an omen of my future college life!" I joked. No one laughed.

Seven long, haunted days later, the college announced that the campus had dried out and the front doors were flung wide open to the thousands—no, hundreds...well, at least several dozen—students who were overdue to continue their education. My devoted, seventy-nine-year-old grandfather drove me three hours down the Florida Turnpike, turned off at the West Palm Beach exit, pulled his golden Lincoln Cadillac to the corner of Dixie Highway and Acacia Street...and stopped. Facing us, just on the other side of the busy main road, stood a large, stone archway bearing the carved title WOODLAWN CEMETERY.

"Where's my dorm?"

Granddaddy shared my confusion. "327 Acacia Street. Corner of Dixie. Yeah, this is it." He began to chuckle. "I think your college got some building numbers mixed up! What kind of a school would make their students live in the graveyard?"

"Well, we must be close, because there are college kids walking all over the place." I called to a passing undergraduate who was armed with a notebook under one arm and a large surfboard in the other. "We're looking for 327 Acacia Street. It's a girls' dorm at PBA. Do you know where it is?"

"You're right in front of it!" The scholarly surfer pointed a few feet in back of our rear window.

"Where?" I argued. "There's nothing here but a bunch of overgrown trees and a run-down old house!"

"That's it! Riddle House. It used to be a funeral parlor, you know."

My grandfather looked as ill as I felt. *This* was where he had spent his life's savings to send me? The rest of the small campus was a bit second-hand, but charming and quite clean. This house, on the other hand, looked worse than its neighboring graveyard.

"He's kidding, Granddaddy!"

"I'm afraid not. 327 Acacia Street is the address, and that house has a big *327* on that porch pillar."

It couldn't be true. Had I escaped a life of paranormal frying pans, only to be plopped right into the fire of another haunted house—and this one next to a cemetery? Was there no escaping these darned haunted houses? I pulled my suitcase out of the Lincoln's trunk and dragged it up the house's wide front porch steps.

I peered through the open front door. Puke green shag carpet, faded from a decade of dirty shoes, had been slapped over the entire ground floor. A faint smell of must, mixed with a twist of stinky summer sweat, permeated the air. The house was smaller than it appeared from the outside, but that may have been due to the dozens of teenage boys who were stuffing themselves into the tiny front parlor, just to the left of the front door.

"I think I have the wrong dorm!" I announced with ecstasy.

"Oh no, you have the right house, Vivian! Your room is the second at the top of the stairs." My new dorm "mom," Rebecca, smiled like Cleopatra in the snake pit.

"But…but, this place is stuffed with *boys*!" I stammered.

"Oh, they're just the welcoming committee." Rebecca shrugged. "For as long as I can remember, all the boys line the front steps of the freshman girls' dorms, and PBA has three of them. Dobbs House is a few blocks down on Vallowe Court, and Weyenberg is in back of Dobbs. They're both a bit bigger, but we like to think that Riddle House has quality rather than quantity."

Oh great. I was to be monitored all year by a cliché-quoting upperclassman.

With a sigh, I dragged my suitcase inside my new home. A short hallway divided the left front parlor from the right front stairway, then lead straight back to the rear of the house, where a closed door displayed the dire warning: "Dorm Parent's Suite. No Admittance." There was no risk of that from me; that part of the house looked even danker than the front. I sidestepped the boys and turned toward the stairs.

The wooden steps twisted up through the center of the small second floor like a misplaced lighthouse stairwell and were so narrow that they admitted only one person at a time. My loyal grandfather, dressed in his best business suit and tie, trudged up after me, one squeaky stair at a time. I wasn't sure if the old house was greeting us or squealing in pain.

The second floor layout turned out to be a tangle of three bedrooms, divided and intertwined by two short hallways and two closed doors.

"Where the heck is the bathroom?" A tall, thin girl, several years older than myself, with peroxided hair and jet black bangs, darted out of an open bedroom and swung open a closed door at the far end of the hall. "Is this the *only* bathroom in the whole house? Oh, my god! This place is a *nightmare!*"

I shot a worried glance at my grandfather. "Let's find your room," he offered. The task wasn't hard: there were only three doors left to choose from. I placed my hand on a glass doorknob next to the bathroom and twisted. The door was dead bolted.

"Don't touch that door!" Rebecca had arrived at the top of the stairs to confirm the bathroom inquiry. "That's just the janitor's closet. We always keep it locked. Viv, your room is over here, down this little hall." I stepped into a sunny, white room, blessed with four wood-paned windows that seemed to stretch from the ceiling to the floor. Against the walls stood two single beds and a pair of old wooden dressers, fresh from the nearest thrift store.

"You can also use this little closet, right outside your door. The adjoining bedroom will use the second little hallway between your connecting rooms as their closet.

Sorry, there's only one bathroom, but there's only six girls in this house, besides me, so I'm sure you'll all work out your shower schedules." Dorm moms apparently got their own private bathroom in their private downstairs suite.

The brochures never mentioned this aspect of college dorm life. Still, despite the odd inconveniences and the regrettable downstairs carpet, the old house had some charm. I supposed anyone who hadn't grown up in older homes would have run straight out the door, but that only led to the graveyard, and even a one-bathroom house seemed preferable to that. I smiled reassuringly at my worried grandfather.

"I'll be fine!"

He cuddled me in a big bear hug. "I know. You're *my* granddaughter!" Neither of us wanted to let go. The only thing that was harder for me than watching him drive away that day was his having to do it by himself. I had the very best grandfather in the whole wide world.

The female freshman sextuplets of Riddle House settled into our century-old home. My roommate, Cindy, was a committed Southern Baptist who dreamed of being an FBI forensic pathologist. For two wonderful weeks, we got along like two peas in a pod, decorating our room and trading midnight stories of our lives and future dreams. We never missed a meal together and lamented that we shared only one class in common this semester. Life with Cindy was good…until the day Dorm Mom Rebecca called me into her private downstairs suite. I was surprised to find my new roommate already seated at the kitchen table.

"Vivian, Cindy and I were wondering if you could help us find some money that she's misplaced."

I was confused. "What are you talking about?"

My roommate jumped to her feet so fast that she nearly knocked over her chair. "You know very well what I'm talking about! I left a pile of change on my dresser when I left for class this morning, and when I came back two hours later, it had disappeared!" Detective Cindy pointed an accusatory finger in my face. "You were the only other person in the whole house this morning. Everyone else had left by nine except you!"

I didn't know whether to laugh or just punch Cindy in her paranoid nose. Who was this raving liar and what had she done with my friendly little roommate? Rebecca took charge of the brewing brawl.

"Why don't we all just go upstairs to your room and look for the money? Cindy, are you sure that you checked all your pockets?"

Our trio marched up the twisted stairway. Cindy led the way into our room and made a beeline for the electric coffee pot that stood on my dresser. "I see my money!" she exclaimed with glee as she lifted the pot. Underneath was Cindy's laundry money: six quarters and a dime.

I couldn't believe it! My new best friend and roomie had set me up! Was she so obsessed with being a detective that she was going to use me as her practice criminal? Rebecca hadn't known either of us long enough to pass judgment, so she just suggested that we both concentrate on keeping our small room as tidy as possible.

A month later, I was back at Rebecca's kitchen table again. This time, Cindy had lost an inexpensive ring. She and Rebecca had elected to ignore college policy and inspected our room while I was in class. They had reportedly found the elusive ring under my coffee pot!

"Oh, for heaven's sake!" I grumbled. "If I was a kleptomaniac, why would I take stupid stuff like plastic rings and laundry coins and constantly stuff them under my coffee pot, especially since Cindy uses that pot all the time?"

There was no logical answer except that one of us was crazy. No one else in the house wanted to switch roommates, so we would have to resolve the problem ourselves or face the dean.

Cindy's green and pink plastic bottle of mascara disappeared next. We found it in the possession of my coffee pot. Every week or so, another small item of my roommate's would rematerialize under that darn pot. Cindy's grades were less than stellar, so she decided to avoid pursuing the matter with college officials, but she sure let the rest of the Riddle House girls know about her thieving roommate! Katrina, the black-and-blonde punk rock hopeful who shared the coveted room next to the bathroom, seemed to be my only ally.

"I know who's taking Cindy's stuff," Kat confided to me one day over the blasts of her B-52's record album. "It's that little girl!"

"What little girl?"

"Haven't you seen her? Of all the people in this house, I thought you would have, for sure, Viv! I don't know her name, but she thinks it's pretty funny how upset Cindy gets when she finds her stupid junk under your coffee pot."

"Kat, what on earth are you talking about? There aren't any kids around here…"

"The *ghost*!"

I was well aware that our graveyard house practically shook with paranormal energy, but I had quickly blocked it out, like a bad smell, as I had learned to do in the past. Occasional childhood exploration aside, ignoring those vibes was the only way to make a haunted house your home, especially if you have classes to concentrate on.

Katrina had a solution: "Hey, come over to that graveyard with me—we'll see if we can figure out if the little girl is buried over there and ask her to stop taking Cindy's stuff!"

"Kat, that graveyard is huge. Even if you knew this ghost's name, there's no way that we'd be able to find her plot or even if she's in there at all. I'm not going into any graveyard. I'm going to class." It seemed wiser to keep my paranormal sensitivities secret at my Southern Baptist college. Kat was rumored to smoke pot, anyway, but I suspected that accusation was just because she was a punk rock fan. As it turned out, Katrina wasn't the only one who knew about our small spirit.

Tracy, a four-eleven self-proclaimed Baptist beauty queen, lived in the bedroom adjoining mine. She had arrived at Riddle House with her six-foot-tall boyfriend, Terry, who dutifully toted her endless array of matching tapestry luggage up and down the narrow stairway. He was going into the ministry, and she was going down the aisle with him just as soon as either of them managed to graduate. "I'm just here for an M.R.S. degree!" she would announce with a twinkle in her eye. Karla, her stout roommate, believed in bathing once a week and reportedly contracted scabies by second semester.

One afternoon, Tracy motioned Katrina and me into her bedroom and shut the door behind us. The Baptist beauty queen looked sick. "I just got grabbed around my legs!"

Katrina and I didn't have a clue in the world what she was talking about. "Did Terry throw you over his shoulder again? Tracy, nobody's in this whole house except us."

" …and that little girl ghost!" The beauty queen was dead serious.

Katrina was elated. "How do you know about her? I thought you were Baptist!"

"Oh, shove it, Kat! Of course I know about her! She's been hanging out in my closet in the middle of my dresses and heels since the first day we moved in! She's a real girly girl—*loves* playing with my makeup."

"Yeah, she likes to steal Cindy's mascara, too," I lamented.

Tracy looked worried. "I was just about to leave my room to meet Terry for lunch, when she suddenly popped in and grabbed me around my legs! She didn't want me to leave!"

"She must really like you," Kat noted with envy. "She never touches me."

"No, Kat, she was *terrified*! She wanted me to protect her from that mean, tall guy."

"What mean, tall guy?"

"That *other* ghost in this house."

Riddle House was getting more crowded by the minute! Thank goodness ghosts didn't use the bathroom.

Tracy was trembling. "He was just in here, too. I can't believe that of everyone in this house, you two missed all this! That poor little girl had me in this vise grip—I was about to lose my balance—when the mean guy popped in behind me and sort of *loomed* over me like a grizzly bear with its claws outstretched."

Katrina and I swept a horrified glance around our friend's cheery bedroom. "Is he still in here?"

"No, he bolted. I just told him to get lost and he went. He won't dare come back in here while I'm around. Problem is, the little girl disappeared, too. I think she's trapped in this house because of him."

A week later, Tracy knocked on my door again. "Did you hear those voices last night?"

"What voices?"

"The little girl and the mean man! They were mumbling all night. I couldn't make out what they were saying, but it sounded like he was angry and she was pleading with him. What am I going to do? I need to get some sleep! I tried earplugs, but they don't help because I can still hear those voices. It's driving me crazy!"

We three agreed to keep the paranormal conversations to ourselves, lest the student body—not to mention boyfriend Terry—would send Tracy to the local loony bin or to an exorcist.

I was baffled by Tracy's description of a "mean man." I was well aware of a male spirit in our house, but the one I knew was gentle and unassuming. Since I'm a night owl whose brain wakes up when the sun goes down, I often tiptoed downstairs to the cozy parlor and did my homework in peace and quiet long after curfew, while everyone else was asleep. It was also the only time that the parlor was empty of boys...except for my spectral friend. I would plop myself and my portable typewriter in front of the tiny black-and-white TV, surround myself with piles of textbooks and papers, and eat a quart of Howard Johnson's pistachio ice cream. And I always made the dean's list.

The first night I heard the footsteps on the stairs, I panicked. Oh, no. If I woke up anyone, especially dorm mom Rebecca, I would be banished from my midnight studies and flunk my freshman year. I leaned out of the doorway and peeked into the dark hall. Thank goodness! Every living person in the house was snoring. No sooner had I returned to my typing than the stairway began creaking with footsteps again. I was terrified. This time, I took a good long look at the stairs.

That's when I finally noticed the man. He was dressed in plain work clothes, like a farmer or a handyman from the early 1900s. He didn't seem to notice me; he stood in the middle of the stairway, caught halfway between up and down. The man just stared straight ahead, lost in his thoughts and time. Poor guy. I returned to my typing.

The walking man became my late-night homework companion. I can't say that we became close friends, because the most attention that he ever paid to me was to occasionally watch me typing away during commercials. He seemed to like watching the TV; our favorite shows were *Fawlty Towers*, *Monty Python's Flying Circus*, and *SCTV*. Most of the time, the ghost would just wander down the stairs, into the hall, into the parlor, back into the hall, and then back up to the second floor. His footsteps always faded away around the top step. I didn't think about where he went. He never bothered me, and I never bothered him. I also never told another living soul about him. Tracy and Katrina had their pet ghost, and I was happy to have mine.

We never found out what happened to that little girl. Tracy and Katrina moved out at the end of the school year, along with their roommates. I had decided to stay on for the summer in order to take to a few extra classes and get a head start on my sophomore year. The college agreed to let me stay at Riddle House until two weeks before the fall semester started, and Cindy was replaced by my new roommate, Annabelle. Annabelle, the walking man ghost, and I spent a happy, peaceful Florida summer together in the old house. None of our personal possessions ended up under the coffee pot and we never heard any voices other than our own—this ghost preferred walking to talking.

That would seem to be the end of the story: six teen-age girls attend a small Christian school and are assigned to live in an old, haunted house next door to an old, haunted graveyard. The local boys tease that the house used to be a funeral parlor with dead bodies stacked up in the front window. The girls meet some resident ghosts, survive, and are promoted to sophomore level. The house falls into disrepair and is reportedly demolished the following year.

But thirty years later, one of the girls is watching a ghost hunting show on TV and is shocked to recognize the house they are investigating: it's her Riddle House dorm, risen from the dead! I was equally shocked to find out that the rumors were true: the 1904 house was the original home of the caretaker for Woodlawn Cemetery, built as security to prevent pesky criminals from exhuming bodies and stealing their personal possessions. To my surprise, history also notes that a gentle graveyard worker, reportedly named Buck, was killed during an argument, and his ghost was often reported wandering around the graveyard. Despite his violent death, Buck's spirit was never seen to be angry or vengeful. He just liked to walk around.

To top that off, I found out that a few years after gentle Buck's demise, another local handyman, reportedly named Joseph, hung himself in the Riddle House attic—the same attic that the college kept behind a permanently locked door, passing it off as a janitor's closet to their innocent freshman girls. The whole scenario sounds like the plot to a B-grade horror flick. At least, all the girls of the Riddle House sure thought so . . . even the invisible ones.

NOTE: Riddle House was saved from demolition at the last minute by John Riddle, the nephew of the house's original owner. The bright yellow building was moved to Yesteryear Village in the West Palm Beach's South Florida Fairgrounds, where it stands today, completely renovated, carefully cared for, and as happily haunted as ever.

four

Honeymoon with the Shadow Man

Atlanta, Georgia:
1991–1993

H e's standing right behind you."

The man was there before we moved in. He was there after we moved out. They say two's company, but I can tell you that three's a horror movie.

Like most newlyweds, Jack and I saw our first apartment together through rose-colored glasses...and we weren't far off. The newest flock of prestigious Post Apartments had transformed yet another quiet cow pasture in the middle of Lawrenceville, Georgia, into the latest outer suburb of Atlanta. What had once been peaceful peach groves and scattered country homes morphed into mega malls and condo clones. Jack and I each worked on Peachtree Street, right in the middle of the bustling big city of Atlanta, so we were thrilled to find an affordable residential haven that was only a forty-five minute car drive plus a twenty minute train ride and a few long escalators away from our jobs. Hey, beggars can't be choosers in crowded Atlanta.

Our second-story apartment was spanking new and spacious, with vaulted ceilings, a glassed-in sunroom, a downstairs bedroom, bathroom, and a winding staircase that lead to a complete suite in the loft. There was plenty of room for us and my new stepson, Ian, who stayed with us on Wednesdays and weekends. What we couldn't figure out was the price. Most monthly rental fees for Post Apartments reflected the rising salary of the single yuppie movers-and-shakers they attracted, but our place cost less than $500 a month, as did the other three apartments in our building. We assumed this was due to the view: while the other buildings in the complex looked onto swimming pools and fountains, the four apartments in our building peeked over a rotting picket fence, gray rooftops, and a parking lot. We were at the back of the complex, next to the garbage bins. The result was that we all lived in top-class apartments for a fraction of the usual price!

Jack was the first to notice the ghost. He was standing in the far corner of Ian's downstairs bedroom when he saw a shadow within a shadow, in the shape of a tall man with no face. In a blink, the image was gone. Since Ian wasn't visiting us on that particular night, Jack decided not to mention his spooky discovery to anyone. It was probably just a trick of the moonlight...although that night was cloudy and the window shades were drawn.

I didn't see the ghost, but I knew the back hall gave me the willies.

"Do you think it's OK to have Ian sleep in that back bedroom?" I asked my new husband one evening.

"Sure. Why not?"

"I dunno. It just feels kinda weird in there. That room seems darker at night than the other rooms."

"Well, the other rooms have higher ceilings," Jack logically argued. "Ian's room is just cozy, that's all."

My instincts argued otherwise, but Ian was Jack's son, and I wanted to respect his parental wishes. Still, when seven-year-old Ian slept over with us, I always made sure that his door was left wide open with the nearby bathroom light left on.

But some ghosts don't like being kept secret, and the black cat jumped out of the bag one evening in January. We were sitting on the couch, talking, when Jack stopped in mid-sentence. His eyes seemed to glaze over as he stared at something behind me. I glanced over my shoulder, saw nothing, and then glanced back at Jack. A weird smile had crossed his face. It gave me the creeps.

"What is it?" I asked. "Is there something in the hall?"

"The hall is empty. He's standing right behind you."

My head whipped around again, but I saw the same empty space in back of me. I jumped to my feet so fast that I forgot I was balancing my half-full coffee cup on my lap. The ensuing stain barely crossed my mind.

"*Who* is in back of me, Jack? Stop smiling like that! You look weird!"

Jack leaned back on the couch. "It's just a man. I've seen him around here a few times."

"Where?" After my lifetime of attracting every passing paranormal pixie, I could hardly believe there was actually a ghost that I couldn't see or sense. The extrasensory tables were turned: for the first time, I had become a Helen Keller to the spirit world and Jack was my savvy Anne Sullivan.

"Oh, he's just standing there. He's smiling at you." Jack spoke as if he was commenting on fair weather.

"Well, tell him to stop it!" I commanded. Jack just smiled.

"I don't think he'll do anything anyone else tells him to do."

I spun around to face the empty air where my Peeping Tom reportedly stood.

"*Go away!*" I screamed.

Jack chuckled. "He's back in the hall doorway now, but he's still looking at you."

I never saw the Shadow Man with my eyes, but after that night, I became intensely aware of his presence. He watched me while I slept. He watched me while I bathed. He haunted the downstairs hallway and lurked in the corner of my young stepson's bedroom. But Ian remained blissfully unaware of his spectral roommate. I guess Jack figured that what Ian didn't know couldn't hurt him. Nonetheless, Jack began sleeping on the downstairs couch next to the hallway during Ian's overnight visits.

We'd lived in the apartment for nearly two years when our next door neighbor, Sheila, knocked on our door.

"You guys are going to think I'm crazy, but, um … well, you know that I live alone with my little boy, Christopher, and I'm just nervous. Christopher has been saying that he sees a dark, tall man made of shadows in his bedroom. Now, Chris is only two and can barely talk, so I just thought it was his imagination getting scrambled with some scary TV show. But, he refuses to sleep in his own bed and has been in mine for over a month now. I finally called my brother, Mick, to come over and check things out for us. Mick slept in Chris's room, which is in our upstairs loft, and … well, Mick saw the man, too!"

Jack and I gulped.

Sheila continued. "Mick's a professional football player, so he's a tough guy, but he was so freaked out by whatever he saw that he insisted on moving in with us to keep us safe from the 'spooky man.' So, I was just wondering if Ian had said anything to you about it. He comes over to play with Chris sometimes."

"Ian doesn't know anything about it," Jack confessed, "but we do. That man is in our apartment, too. He's a ghost."

Sheila's jaw dropped out. "He's in your place, too? That's crazy! How can he haunt two apartments at once? Does he just walk through the walls? And why is he here in the first place? This isn't some old Louisiana plantation. This complex is only about five years old and there was just a field here for decades before that."

"Who knows," Jack shrugged. "I wouldn't worry about it too much. The ghost isn't doing anyone any harm. He's just kind of spooky."

I jumped into the conversation: "Jack, he *watches* me all the time! I woke up with some weird marks on my shoulder the other day. He turns the bedroom TV off and on all the time and watches me when you're sleeping on the downstairs couch, trying to keep an eye on Ian. This is nuts. There has to be some way to get rid of him."

The next day, Sheila and I knocked on the door of our downstairs neighbor, Gary, who was the first tenant in our five-year-old building. It turned out that not only was Gary well acquainted with our wandering Shadow Man, but he had a theory of how he ended up haunting the place …

"There was a big family that lived in Jack and Viv's apartment before them. They told the apartment manager that there were only five people on their lease, but there were easily thirteen or fourteen folks living in there at any one time. They had little kids and babies and grandmas and every age in between. I don't think half of them were blood related. Anyhow, they practiced Santería."

I could hardly believe my ears! "They practiced what? Santa—what? Is that some kind of voodoo?"

"No. Santería is a religion that came out of western Africa and the Caribbean. Some people mistake it for voodoo, but it's different. I don't know a lot about it, but since I lived in the apartment right underneath them, I can tell you that I was kept awake many a night with the sounds of drumming and dancing. One time, I saw a couple of people drive up in the middle of the night with some live chickens. I saw them carry those hens up to your apartment, Viv, but I never saw those chickens again. Now, maybe they were just having a late-night supper of fried chicken. All I know is they were dancing up there 'til the sun came up."

"So, you're saying that animal sacrifices were performed in my living room?!"

Gary shrugged. "I can't say, but the manager had your whole apartment re-carpeted after those folks moved out. I never told on those upstairs renters, but I guess someone else did, because after a couple of months, the manager finally tossed them out for having too many people living there. One of the workmen who was in there told me he saw something like a fire pit hole cut in the center of the living room, and there were weird stains and burn marks on the carpet, too."

"Didn't anyone call the police on them for disturbing the peace so late at night?" Sheila wondered.

"I never saw any cops. There wasn't anyone else in this building at that time except us. The other two apartments were vacant … at least, they were supposed to be. Sheila, I hate to tell you this, but I'm fairly sure that I saw some of those Santería people coming out of your place, too. They probably picked the lock. There was no way they could have fourteen people living in Viv's apartment and still have room for an altar in the living room."

Sheila shook her head. "So, you think those Santería people did something to call up the Shadow Man?"

Gary shrugged. "I first saw him show up in my back bedroom a few days after the new carpet was laid in the empty upstairs unit. He pops up now and then, but I just ignore him. The rent on this place is way too sweet to pass up on account of a ghost … or whatever he is. Hoodoo says that if you don't believe in something, then it can't hurt you. I figure the same thing applies to our ghost."

Gary's story confirmed my worst fears. Although I had no idea that any type of magic or animal sacrifice had happened in our apartment, I had always felt that this "ghost" was actually some kind of an evil spirit taking the form of a human. It just felt different than most of the other ghosts that I had run into in the past. We had to get little Ian out of that cursed apartment...but, where else could we afford to move? I prayed every day for an answer.

One week later, my darling grandfather called from Orlando and my prayers were answered. It had been almost twenty years since he and Grandma had moved to an apartment from the house my family had shared with them until 1970. He allowed his elderly missionary friends to become the house's caretakers while they took care of their octogenarian mother, Grace. Contrary to her doctor's dire predictions, Grace's birthday cake held one hundred candles before her soul left this earth and rose happily to heaven. After the missionaries finally moved out, Granddaddy offered his house to my parents, but they felt that it was too big for them to take care of at their age, so he rang my phone in Atlanta, instead.

"Ten dollars and it's all yours, Viv! The yard, the house, and everything in it." His voice twinkled with happiness. "The money's just to make it legal, y'know."

It was a domestic dream come true. Our family would have a house! The very next day, Jack and I put in our final notice to our Atlanta employers. Two weeks later, when Ian arrived to spend his spring break vacation with us, we grabbed a bottle of sunblock, stuffed Ian and my ornery cat, Black Magic, in the car, and left the Shadow Man alone to haunt the next unsuspecting tenant of apartment 216.

five

Unexpected
Guests

Orlando, Florida:
1993–1995

April 1, 1993

Edgar Allen Poe would have envied the night. The full moon spilled rays of silver over spider webs of Spanish moss hanging from ancient live oaks like corpses. Only the old house ignored the moonshine, looming in one great shadow over its weed-choked yard as it had for almost seven decades.

I glanced down at my watch. It was exactly midnight, April Fool's Day.

My grandfather's massive house had stood proudly in the heart of old Orlando since 1927. My mother was only twelve when it became our family homestead in 1940. My Scottish great-grandfather spent the last years of his life in the small upstairs bedroom that would later become mine and eventually my elder daughter's. My parents were married under the archway in the front room and celebrated their first anniversary by planting the graceful Magnolia tree that carpeted the front yard with a snowfall of giant white blossoms every May, just in time for my birthday.

The grand house had suffered with age. Its fairy tale casement windows had been ripped out and replaced with stark aluminum frames. The roof's olive oval shingles were now dirty red slates. In the 1950s, its sleek stucco exterior had been slathered with a tan cement-based permanent "protective coating," leaving the house with a bumpy skin disease. Despite the physical insults, the house's charm never waned. No one could pass by the old place without stopping to gaze up at its gently sloping gables and magnificent live oaks. You could feel the memories. "What a great house! Somebody should really fix it up." The boomtown showplace of the 1927 neighborhood was now the eyesore of the block.

It had been almost twenty years since my grandfather moved out of this house and into nearby Lucerne Towers

Apartments, allowing a family of elderly missionaries to become its live-in caretakers in lieu of rent. Four months after my grandfather's friends finally moved out, my husband and I drove from Atlanta to Orlando with my stepson to claim my beloved family home.

Greenwood Street's craggy red brick street greeted us as I turned the last corner with my family in tow. The street lamps seemed to dim as the jagged silhouette of the old roof peeked out between two centuries of oaks. At the end of the block, the house sprung up at us like a phantom grizzly bear. I was horrified. What had happened to my charming early-childhood home? The house was as it always had been, yet as it never had been. Gloom twisted through every familiar board and brick. A disease of black mist hung over it like a tattered shawl. Even the moon's light seemed to disappear when I looked at the scary house that was to be our home.

No one breathed as I slowly steered my little Ford Escort up the driveway. We melted into the great lurking shadow of the towering house. Unpacking was out of the question. Even setting foot outside the car was unthinkable. We sat in the car, mesmerized with fear. Not even my cantankerous cat dared to mew.

"Come on out, everybody!" Immune to the gloom and late hour, my exuberant dad, who lived only a mile away, had decided to welcome us at the front door. I cringed and sank down behind the steering wheel, certain that a bathrobed posse of rudely awakened neighbors would dash out to lynch him. I admit that my father had a right to be proud. In his excitement about my moving back to Orlando, he had organized a cleaning crew to scrub the place. This was no easy task; the vacated house hadn't seen a vacuum cleaner in months. The Disaster Relief Fund would have turned down my dad's plea for aid. Fortunately, several of his stout-hearted friends joined in and bravely waged war on the mold, mildew, and dust bunnies. When they finished, the house was spotless.

A familiar wooden groan shook the night: Daddy had swung open the massive front door, which looked like an appropriated castle drawbridge. The moat dried up, so the job boss stuck it on the front of our house instead.

That sound meant time was up. No more car asylum. I took a breath, opened my car door, and walked toward my childhood home. A slew of Arctic air bellowed out of the open doorway and straight into my face.

"When did we get central air in the house?" I asked as I poked my head into the dark front room. "I thought we could barely afford electric fans."

My dad laughed. "What are you talking about? This place doesn't have central anything, except a few mice and lizards in the walls. Let me find the light switch in here …" Daddy sprang toward the nearest wall and groped around. With a sharp click, a dim yellow beam of light glowed from one of the eight ancient wall sconces that lined the room.

I allowed myself a short breath of relief. The front room looked just like I remembered it, even if it felt like Alcatraz. The once-alabaster walls, now yellowed with age, still shouldered eight massive wooden beams that criss-crossed the ceiling, English cottage style. A small, broken piece of corner beam caught my eye; I peered closer and discovered that it had been Scotch-taped back into place. The gray metal gas floor heater that had blocked the fireplace for the past fifty years still emitted acrid fumes and looked twice as ugly as it smelled.

"That thing has got to go!" I whispered to Jack. My husband held his nose and nodded. I could hardly believe how scarred my poor old house had become over the past twenty years since my family had last occupied it. Despite its recent cleaning, the residue of heat, humidity, and elderly humans obstinately refused to depart. The stately outer walls were pockmarked and peeling, four cracked windows were pierced by ancient air conditioner units, and tears of dried black slime streamed down the yellowed walls. Even its sturdy lath-and-plaster bones bore cracks of house-osteoporosis.

To my amazement, every piece of furniture stood in exactly the same place it had when I was a child, despite the fact that another family had lived here for the past two decades. I lovingly ran my hand over the smooth arm of my grandfather's favorite black leather rocker, still sadly wondering why its owner had deserted it twenty years ago. I couldn't imagine anyone other than

Granddaddy sitting in it. Over in the corner, my great-grandmother's rosewood piano still stood sentry beside her red velvet, nineteenth-century love seat. How many times had I curled up there while my mother played her favorite "Clair de lune"? The house would ring with her music and the ghosts would fly away.

Shaking my head in dismay, I walked toward the gently peaked curves of the Turkish-styled open archway that lead into the dining room. Six Depression-era dinette chairs, each painted a different vibrant color, congregated around the bare wooden table while a somber painting of a gnarled old man bowing over his last crust of bread scowled overhead. Given the vibe in this place, I wondered if he was pleading with God for food or an exorcist.

We followed my father from room to room, frantically turning on every craggy chandelier and light bulb we could find. Silence deafened our whispers. A neatly dusted wall calendar stubbornly marked the days of 1983. *Time is frozen here*, I realized with horror. No clocks worked. None of the withered family photos that hung on the walls were newer than 1940; most of them were tintypes of my long-dead ancestors as children. In the center of the hallway hung a yellowed, dog-eared snapshot of myself at about four years old happily sitting in our front yard, a sea of lilac lace ruffles on Easter morning. "I'm the only living member of my family pictured in this house," I whispered. *Who had hung my photo here?*

In addition to the sienna family photographs, many of my wealthy ancestors' paintings also decorated the walls, their once-bright oils now darkened with age and their gold baroque frames pitted with chunks of fallen plaster. My great-grandmother, Jenny Andre, a talented artist, was the pioneer daughter of a nineteenth-century Colorado silver miner, and much of her work reflected the harsh Rocky Mountain climate, such as the somber portrait of a skeletal caribou collapsed and dying in a bleak snowdrift. This morbid painting hung right beside the dining room table.

One picture that my great-grandmother did not create was a mammoth canvas entitled "De l'Infante Marguerite." It was a century-old portrait copy of a young medieval Spanish princess. From her expression, I suspected the child was demon-possessed. She was depicted as a solemn little girl with large, sinister eyes that pierced straight through yours as you looked at her. This huge painting hung at eye level at the bottom of the staircase; from this vantage point, Marguerite could watch you through half of the house. Her oily yellow eyes followed you everywhere, even when you couldn't see her. As a child, I had been certain that she would pop out of her frame and throttle me; looking at it as an adult, I realized my childhood fears hadn't been unjustified.

However, the house was filled with more than eccentric family mementos. From the moment we stepped through the front door, Jack and I felt like two small insects stalked by an invisible can of Raid. Something wanted us out, something that we couldn't see. The second floor felt as if something had sucked out the oxygen. Out of polite deference to my dad, we forced ourselves to quickly peek through the upper bedroom doorways, then stampeded back down the stairs.

"Jack, don't you think we'd better all sleep together in the downstairs bedroom?" I sputtered as I barreled down the steps.

"Absolutely!" Jack had already flashed past Marguerite at the bottom of the stairs and was halfway out the front door, presumably to unpack our cars.

My poor dad had no idea what was wrong with us, and he was obviously hurt that we didn't share his enthusiasm. "But, I already made up the upstairs bedrooms for you guys!" he pleaded in astonishment. "I bought brand-new pillows and sheets. There are only bedspreads on those two beds downstairs. We'll have to dig out more sheets for them and I don't know if the blankets are clean ..."

"No problem!" I chirped, grabbing a pile of linen from a nearby closet. My stomach ached with guilt. Daddy had gone to so much trouble for us, but I didn't know how to explain our problem to him. My skeptical father was always less than sympathetic on the subject of ghosts.

"Daddy, you've done an amazing job cleaning this place and we can never thank you enough for all you've done for us. We're just too tired to lug all our suitcases up these stairs tonight. We'll get settled in later." Thankfully, my dad chose to buy my weak rationalization and sweetly followed me to help organize our family bedroom for the night.

The first floor's "new" bedroom suite and connecting bathroom had been added in 1961 by my grandfather after my grandmother's weak heart prevented her from climbing the stairs. Four great windows welcomed as much sunshine as possible into her remaining days. One of my favorite photos was of Granddaddy holding me as a baby, cheek-to-cheek, as we peeked out of one of those half-finished cement-block windows. Thirty years later, I gazed out of that same dusty glass and wished it was 1961 again.

With a resolved sigh, I returned to the grim present and helped my dad tuck a sky-blue sheet over one of the matching double beds. Like the rest of the house, this room was still virtually unchanged and held my grandmother's original bedroom suite: two double beds, several dressers, two nightstands and a bookcase crammed with Reader's Digest condensed books. I could almost smell her Camay soap. The same rose-and-gold comb and brush set that used to glide through her wavy silver-blond hair lay on her dressing table. I picked up her hand mirror, hoping to catch her reflection smiling reassuringly. Only my own pale face stared back.

"Vivian, this house is kind of spooky." Ten-year-old Ian struggled to pull an overstuffed suitcase twice his weight through the bedroom door.

"I know, sweetie," I answered, grabbing the luggage from him, "but it'll feel better in the morning after we have a good sleep and get settled in. Sunshine changes everything. I promise."

I dumped the baggage on the nearest bed and sent him scampering back to the car in search of Black Magic's kitty water dish.

As soon as Ian left the room, my dad scowled at me. "You've filled that poor little boy's head full of your sick ghost stories!"

"I am not sick!" I hotly retorted, trying to mask my hurt feelings. "And this house is haunted! You seem to be the only person here who can't feel it! You know, I'm not the only one who's told stories about this place. There was my college friend, Samantha …"

Daddy snorted. "If you don't like this beautiful old house, then why did you move back in?"

I was beginning to wonder that myself, but I bit my lip and continued making up the beds in silence. My dad and I always loved each other very much and there was no reason to have an argument neither of us could win. Everyone was getting short-tempered from exhaustion; it was best to follow my own advice and just get some sleep.

By two a.m., the car was empty and the front room was an impasse of junk that Jack and Ian had quickly tossed inside. Daddy hugged everyone goodbye, promising to return at dawn's early light, which was so near that I wondered if the sunrise would beat him to his apartment door.

I settled my cat in the kitchen, locked the front door, and crawled into bed. Jack was already snoring in the double bed next to the window, with Ian snuggled in the matching bed near the door. I staggered into bed beside Jack and yanked my half of the blanket over my aching head. The blessed silence was shattered by Ian's small voice:

"Vivian, aren't you going to turn out the light?"

The light. *Good grief, do I have to turn it off? Oh, wait! I'm the adult here, right?* Putting on my best "brave parent" mask, I crossed the bedroom and switched off the dressing table lamp. Something was wrong. The dark was too thick; too suffocating. I was back into bed in half a hop. "Jack," I whispered to my husband beside me, "don't you think that Ian ought to sleep in bed with us tonight? I mean, is he going to be okay? The room feels kind of … odd."

Jack answered with a snore. Ian was now snoring even louder than his father. Every living thing in the house seemed to be dead asleep, except me.

I gazed over at my stepson's sleeping form to reassure myself that he was safe. Something moved near the wall beside him. I blinked, then blinked again. It was still there. Floating about three feet above the floor was a brownish cloud. *Either that's the world's biggest dust bunny or I'm more exhausted than I thought!* I rationalized to myself. I rubbed my eyes. The cloud wasn't luminous, but opaque and visible against the dark. I desperately wanted to turn on the light, but I didn't want to disturb the sleeping boys. On the other hand, I couldn't take any chances with Ian's safety. What to do? I considered my original plan of moving Ian into our bed, but what on earth would I say if he woke up and saw that foggy thing floating around? The only choice was to physically place myself between Ian and the spooky vapor. I crawled onto Ian's bed and gently rolled my slumbering stepson away from that hovering cloud. It seemed to be a spectral spy observing us, neither sinister nor welcoming. Whatever it was, I had no intention of getting any closer to it.

As I lay there watching the cloud watch me, I was reminded of another night long ago that I spent with a spook in this house before we moved to Lookout Mountain. I was eight years old, Christmas Eve, 1969. That was the night that I saw what I would always call the Face …

Like every other kid around the world on that magical night, I was wide, wide awake, mentally unwrapping every red-and-green present that was waiting for me under the Christmas tree. From my bedroom at the top of the stairs, I could hear every sound that echoed through the big house: I listened to my mother walk into her bedroom down the hall from mine, then my grandfather closed his door downstairs, then much, much later the big TV in the front room went silent and I heard my father's heavy footsteps sleepily move up the stairs and into his bedroom at the end of the hall. In a few minutes, his monstrous snores shook the house.

Suddenly, it wasn't fun to be the only person awake; it was scary! There was only one thing to do: I jumped out of bed and tiptoed down the hall to my mother's room. I knew my way around the big old house well enough to walk it blindfolded, so making my way down the short hall in the dark was no big deal. Closing the door quietly behind me, I slid into the twin bed opposite hers. I could just make out the outline of my sleeping mother, but that was enough to reassure me that now it was safe to go to sleep. Bedroom goblins were always scared of parents. I rolled over on my right side and was about to close my eyes when I happened to glance at the closed door. I should have kept my eyes shut.

Floating in front of the bedroom door, only a few feet away, a glowing demonic face sneered viciously at me. Its long, pointed nose and matching chin dripped halfway down the length of the door; its jagged mouth stretched so wide that it jutted across its face like a bone through a cannibal's nose. Worst of all were its beady, murderous eyes. Grinning like Satan's Cheshire Cat, it beamed milky-white, slowly stretching up and down, then side to side like melting rubber. It was Hell with a face, and it was looking straight at me.

It didn't matter that I was too terrified to move because the Face blocked both the bedroom door and the room's only light switch. I wanted to scream for my mother, but I didn't dare. In the first place, she probably wouldn't be able to see the Face anymore than she saw the other paranormal "things" that I tried to point out to her. More importantly, I feared for her safety. Who knew what the Face might do if I woke Mama up? It was vicious-looking; it might attack anyone who dared move. For the rest of that long night, the disembodied glowing visage silently dared me to stick even one toe out of bed. We never took our eyes off each other.

Somehow Christmas morning managed to dawn. A faint jingling sound from the direction of the bedroom window diverted my eyes momentarily from the Face just as the first rays of the day kissed the darkness away. When I looked back, the Face was slowly beginning to fade, though not as quickly as the surrounding shadows. Long after it had finally disappeared completely, I could still feel its icy leer hovering by the door.

Twenty-two years later, I again found myself locked in a spectral staring contest. I had no intention of closing even one eyelash with that cloud-thing floating around. Sleep was not an option tonight. I had to guard my sleeping boys.

The hours crept by and the day's drive started to take its toll. My anvil eyelids closed for a quick blink. Must not sleep …

With a great yawn, I forced my eyes back open, only to be blinded by blazing sunlight. I sat up in bed and rubbed my face in confusion. Had my best sentinel intentions been defeated by sleep after all? The clock on my bedside table announced that it was 9:45 a.m. Ian's laughter rang through the neighborhood as he raced outside in hot pursuit of a lizard. The familiar breakfast scents of coffee and burned English muffins crawled under the door. Morning had arrived.

Neither Jack nor Ian ever asked why I had suddenly changed beds in the middle of that first night. Maybe they didn't want to know.

One Week Later

"Just pile all those boxes in the master bedroom upstairs."

The moving man raised a bushy eyebrow in question at me. "All of these boxes, ma'am? There's quite a few here. Pretty much took up the back half of m'truck. I put all these up in that one room; won't be no way for you to sleep up there."

"Yep. Thanks."

There was no end to our excuses for not sleeping in any of the bedrooms on the second floor: the rooms needed painting, the lathe and plaster walls had to be mended, and now the master bedroom was conveniently filled with fifty giant moving boxes! Procrastination was our cowards' shield, protecting us from admitting that we had a haunted house on our hands.

Most of the rooms had not been painted since my grandparents purchased the place in 1940. Cracks ran over the walls like spider webs, and spider webs ran over the walls like cracks. Peeling paint made the dirty, cream-colored walls look like decaying birch bark that fluttered onto the fossilized hardwood floors if touched. We couldn't imagine that anything worse could happen to our poor house.

Then the doors began to slam.

BLAM!

Morning, noon, or night, the entire building would suddenly shake with sonic booms, as if a ballistic giant was taking out his temper tantrum on our doors. Days would go by blissfully without so much as a creak, and then the sound of slamming doors would pound through the hallways like a hurricane. We initially dismissed the problem to drafts—F5 tornado drafts that invisibly pummeled our poor doors on dead calm days when not even a twig twitched outside. Sure. Darned drafts.

Logic screamed in terror when faced with the solid fact that no matter how fast we flew to the noise, every single door always remained solidly open at the exact angle at which we'd last seen it, quiet as lambs before Passover. We scrambled for a rational answer.

Experiment #1: Slam each door individually to find out how wide it would bounce back open.

Result: No matter how hard or softly we pushed, they always swung back shut.

Experiment #2: Fortify every door with piles of six-inch-thick books that not even Dwayne "The Rock" Johnson could budge.

Result: Not one door moved a millimeter, even when the earthquake slams caused pictures to slide from the walls.

Experiment #3: Forget experimenting.

"I want to hear the doors slam by themselves!" my friend Lucy moaned. "You always have ghost stories, but never any ghosts around as proof." Lucy had a right to be peeved. She had been my best friend since we were children and had practically grown up in this spooky house with me, but she had never been blessed with so much as a boo.

"Show me the ghost, Vivian!"

My eyes rolled over in dismay. "I never said we had a ghost! I just said that we keep hearing these stupid doors slam. Of course, they never bother to actually budge an inch in our presence; the ear-splitting sound always conveniently occurs in whatever part of the house we aren't in at the time. The second-floor slamming stops the minute we start up the stairs; the ground floor shuts up when we walk down. The only sure way to ensure absolute peace is to invite guests over. Guess why you're here, Lucy!"

Disappointed, Lucy picked up her purse and walked toward our front door. "Invite me back when you have a ghost to introduce!"

Oh boy, I thought. *She ought to be careful what she wishes for.*

Jack sunk happily into the soft depths of our mammoth sofa with three pillows under his head and his legs flung over the arm. The house was dark, save for the flickering blue light from the TV set. His favorite show blared at top volume. Jack wasn't deaf; he was in denial. The set's ear-splitting screech almost obliterated the incessant SLAM! BAM! WHAM! of the upstairs doors. Almost, but not quite. Every time another door slammed, Jack would turn up the sound; every time Jack turned up the sound, the doors would do him one better. Our serene Sunday evening had exploded into a noisy standoff between Jack and the doors.

Across the room, I was blinded by a stabbing sinus migraine. With my back to Jack's glowing TV screen, I nursed my throbbing head in the comforting arms of my grandfather's plump recliner. Just as its soothing magic had begun to work, the upstairs exploded into a roar of wild slamming, as if the entire house was on a suicidal mission to shake itself—and our bursting eardrums—apart. I clamped my hands over my pounding ears and prayed that every door and TV set would disintegrate. Jack cranked up the volume one more time. Could it get any louder?

The din turned me into a rabid tiger.

"Enough, already!"

I leapt from my chair, stomped up the stairs, and planted myself in the center of the murky, narrow hallway. As usual, the doors surrounding me were suddenly as quiet as kids caught with a firecracker. I didn't care. I knew the game. Fire could have shot from my eyes as I accused each doorway, one by one: "All right, I've had it! My head hurts, and I'm tired of this! *Stop it!*" I turned on my heel and marched back downstairs. No sooner had my foot touched the bottom step when—BAM! One more defiant door stubbornly thumbed its nose at me.

My temper exploded into a bonfire of blind fury. Scaling two and three steps at a time, I raced back up into the hall and screamed at the obstinate darkness, "*I said to shut up! I don't want to hear another door slam ever again! Not ever!*" I stood shaking with rage, daring even a termite to nibble in my direction. With one last murderous look at my empty upstairs, I stomped back down the stairway with enough force to shake the walls. Even l'Infante Marguerite shrunk back as I passed her portrait. "And *you* go out in the trash heap tomorrow, tramp!" I bellowed into her yellow eyes.

Jack and his TV were speechless as I collapsed back to my armchair.

"Hey! My headache's gone," I grinned victoriously. Suddenly I knew how Crazy Horse felt holding Custer's bloody scalp.

Marguerite was unceremoniously hauled away by an unsuspecting antique dealer the next day. No door ever dared slam again on its own. Not in *my* house!

Summer 1993

It could have been a shadow. It could have been the heat. Whatever it was, it watched Jack.

He had been painting for hours. Buckets of sweat and peach-colored paint slithered down his ears and neck. Every muscle in his arms and back screamed like an open wound in salt water. Jack painted and painted. Two or three times during that hot afternoon he had glanced back over his shoulder, certain that he was being watched, even though he was alone in the house. Once he thought he caught a glimpse of a smoky form, but when he turned fully around, the room was empty. He dismissed his paranoia to the lack of central air conditioning in the stifling room.

Jack squinted against the sunlight that flooded through the open window and took a step back to critique a wall that had just devoured its fifth layer of paint. Jack jumped back. He blinked. He blinked again. His eyes were playing tricks on him … right?

The man's shadow—or was it a shadowy man?—towered nearly a foot higher than the top of Jack's paint-spattered forehead. Standing tall as a soldier at full attention, it stared at Jack, unabashed and curious. In half a blink, the dark form darted to the right and disappeared behind the heavy barrister bookcase that had been pulled three inches away from the solid wall.

It's a burglar! Jack's brain screamed. Holding his quivering paint brush toward the empty wooden bookshelf, he challenged the intruder.

"Look, I don't have time to play hide-and-seek! Come out from there right now or I'm calling the cops!"

Not a speck of dust moved in reply. Jack peeked behind the bookcase. No one was there. Not a burglar, not a shadow. It wasn't even dark.

Jack had two choices. The first was to throw his paintbrush in the air and run screaming out the front door. The second was to finish painting the room. With a sigh, Jack plunged his brush into a bucket.

"Dumb ghost," he sighed.

The staircase loomed before me like a tunnel to Hades. For weeks, all of my unpacked moving boxes had remained stacked and undisturbed on our haunted second floor. I either had to climb those stairs or spend the remainder of my life wondering what the rest of my earthly belongings looked like. I placed one foot on the first ancient step and shuddered: I was standing under the spot where demonic Marguerite's portrait had resided only a month before. The unpainted plaster wall still retained the smoky brown stain outlining where her frame had stood sentry for the past twenty-two years. Her evil, yellow-eyed ghost still watched, daring me to take a second step. I grabbed the stairwell's black banister in a white-knuckled grip, my fingernails digging into its thick, waxy surface. *Yuck.* With a jagged breath, I started my ascent. Only a month before, I'd charged up these same stairs like a SWAT team to silence the slamming doors; now I was walking on egg-shells, terrified of alerting anything of my arrival. Each wooden step creaked and cackled at my predicament. I felt like an intruder in my own home.

As I rounded the final, third stairway landing, I paused on the top step and peered into the hallway before me. Nothing was out of place. All the doors stood politely open and silent, just as I had left them a month ago.

I closed my eyes and concentrated, straining to feel even a glint of that suffocating fear that turned the pit of my stomach to ice. Amazingly, the air felt clear. No doom and gloom! For the first time since we had moved in, I could breathe upstairs without reminding myself to do so. Hysterical with joy, I dashed from room to room, each one friendlier than the last. The little pink bedroom I slept in for the first years of my life radiated warmth and joy; the old metal adding machine and mahogany desk in Granddaddy's study glowed with excitement. Even the slimy green bathroom grinned. By some miracle, my house—my *real* home—had returned.

I felt like the Salvation Army conquering Skid Row as I marched down the hall, straight into the master bedroom, and ripped the first moving box open with my bare hands, paper cuts be darned! Twelve hours later I was still digging deep into packages and crates, never noticing nor caring that the piles looked no smaller. Tranquility saturated my soul. I started to wonder why we had ever suspected that this beautiful old house was haunted in the first place. So what if the doors slammed for a while; they had quit, right? Every old house had quirks just like every family has a crazy Aunt Mabel who wears plastic grocery bags on her head when it's raining. All Aunt Mabel and this house needed was love and understanding—and a complete face lift.

I glanced behind me. The adjacent unlit bedroom no longer looked just dark; it was pitch black. I swore I could almost make out a form that was darker than the surrounding darkness. A young Caucasian woman with black hair and a long dark dress stood in the empty doorway. I felt as if I was recalling the face of someone far away, but I knew what my eyes saw in that doorway was neither a memory nor imagination. The invisible woman was real and standing in the room with me.

Ignore her, I sternly thought to myself. *Jack's right; we have no time to play games with ghosts. If she wants to watch me work, then let her! Better yet, why doesn't she clear out a closet and help me find someplace to put all this junk?* With an indignant toss of my head, I turned my attention back to the nearest moving box.

Before I had time to blink, something charged across the room and hit my back like a cannonball. My breath whooshed out, my knees buckled, and I hit the hardwood floor. Gasping, I felt an icy pressure gripping my back. I looked up, horrified to see that I was sliding toward the open hallway door! *This can't be real*, my scattered thoughts screamed. I shoved the rubber heel of my tennis shoe against the wooden floor and rolled over to my right, out of the ghost's grip.

I struggled to regain my balance. It was time to flee the entire second floor and cozy up under my blanket at the other end of the house. As I crawled to my feet, the brightly gleaming wall sconce caught my eye. Maybe I couldn't sleep in my old bedroom, but no belligerent spook was going to jack up my electric bill! I attempted a nonchalant stroll across the room to turn off the light.

Pride has always been my Waterloo. The moment I clicked off the light, the bad-tempered phantom ballooned at me with twice its former strength and rage. This time, not only was I shoved out of the bedroom, but also through the hall and straight down the first short flight of stairs. As I hit the mid-curve landing, I grabbed the railing's corner post, hurled myself down the remaining stairs, and landed in a heap on the ground floor. From the top of the stairs, the wraith stared down at my crumpled form. I returned her glare, eye to eye. My family had lived

in this house for fifty-two of its sixty-seven years. If anyone had claim to it, it was me! Still, I decided retreat was
the best course of action that night. It was late, and I'd
had enough unpacking for one day.

The next morning—in the light of day—I decided to
clean out the closets on the second floor.

I began with the smallest closet, which happened to
be located in my pink childhood bedroom. Like the rest of
the house, this room sprouted multiple doors that opened
into other rooms, often with frustrating results. For some
absurd reason, the hall door and the closet door shared
an adjoining corner and opened out toward each other;
when both of these were opened at the same time, their
antique glass doorknobs hooked onto each other, which
always resulted in door gridlock and smashed fingers.

My old closet was somewhat deep but very narrow,
so I had to leave its door wide open while I knelt down
to scrub the bottom shelf, first making certain that the
catty-corner door leading to the hall was shut tight so as
not to risk tangling the contrary doorknobs. No sooner
had my dust cloth touched down when BUMP! The
closet door slammed firmly shut behind me, hitting my
backside and knocking me headfirst into a dust heap
against the rear wall. It would have been comical had my
sense of humor not disappeared in the tiny closet's complete darkness. Rubbing my bruised bottom, I removed
my smashed knees from my ears and groped for the
inner door knob. It wouldn't budge. I shoved my shoulder

against the stubborn door, but just as it started to open a few inches, it slammed shut again. WHAM! Something solid was firmly pressing against the closet door from the outside, trying to keep me trapped inside the closet. It had to be Jack.

My second thrust managed an opening just wide enough to entangle the closet doorknob around the hall doorknob. Wonderful. That door had been opened in the meantime, as well. With a rude WHUMP I was bounced back into the closet again.

My patience was long gone. "Hey!" I yelled. "I'm in the closet and you keep shutting me in. Close that hall door long enough to let me out!" In response to my pleas, the door smashed into my nose. I leaned fully against the obstinate door and gave one great push. The door flew open so fast that I tumbled headlong onto the bedroom floor. The hall door was shut tight as if it had never moved an inch. Steaming mad, I threw it open and loudly demanded, "Why couldn't you have just waited for one second?!" The hallway and stairs were silent, dark and completely empty.

"Jack?"

I glanced into the other rooms. No Jack. No anyone. I charged downstairs and followed the faint sound of the shower running. Feigning bravery, I peeked into the steamy bathroom. A foggy form stood inside the closed stall.

"Jack?" I gulped. There was no answer. "Jack, can you hear me in there?"

The shower's glass door flew wide open.

"Vivian? Did you say something?" Under a heavy stream of scalding water stood my drenched husband, shampoo bubbles skating over his tightly shut eyes. How had he managed to jump into the shower so fast? It was on a different floor and at the opposite end of the house from the closet. Jack's pruned skin looked as if he'd been soaking in the bathroom for an hour.

"Jack, were you trying to get into the pink bedroom upstairs just now? I was cleaning the closet in there."

"No," he shouted over the running water, "I'm taking a shower. Why?"

Nervous sweat beaded my brow as my tangled fingers raced across the computer's keyboard. It was 4:10 p.m. at the local law firm of Hadley, Burns & Barrow. I had twenty minutes to finish typing a brief, sprint two blocks down Orange Avenue, and get it filed before the clerk's office closed in twenty minutes. A passing attorney had tossed his towering mass of legal papers on my desk on his merry way out the door to catch a Friday afternoon golf game. Sometimes it was tough being a legal assistant.

My desk phone rang. The ticking clock, inching ever nearer to my four thirty deadline, suggested that I only pause long enough to toss my inconsiderate telephone out the window. Like a dutiful employee, I picked up the receiver. It was Jack.

"Hi, Viv. I'm at home. I, uh..." He cleared his throat nervously. "I called to tell you about the air conditioner."

Ordinarily my husband's calls were the highlight of my day. This was the wrong day.

"What about it?" I snapped. "Jack, I'm sorry, but I'm really busy right now."

Jack ignored my attitude. "Just a second ago I was in the living room when, um, the window electric air conditioner unit suddenly came on."

Now that was news! Cold air at last! "You mean you fixed it? I can't believe it! That thing is older than Methuselah. I don't remember even Granddaddy getting it to work. What did you do?"

Jack gulped. "I didn't do a thing. I never touched it. I just walked in the room and it came on full blast—and it wasn't even plugged in!"

Ah, great. Our post-living residents had returned from their summer vacation.

"Oh well, I guess the ghosts felt hot, too!" I joked. Jack didn't laugh. I bade him goodbye and resumed typing. My phone rang again. It was Jack.

"I just walked upstairs to the study. Guess what happened?"

I couldn't care less. "Jack, I really have to get this stupid brief finished..."

"I sat down at the desk next to the file cabinet and suddenly the drawers started flying open and shut. They're still doing it right now as we speak. Vivian, I tell you, I'm standing here, wide awake, watching file drawers open and shut by themselves!"

"Jack, I am in an infinitely more terrifying situation. As we speak, the head attorney is standing beside my chair, glaring at me because I'm on a personal call with a half-typed brief that should have been finished and filed yesterday! Good-bye!"

"Wait!" Jack pleaded, "They stopped! Only the bottom drawer is standing open now."

I sighed. "Well, I guess the ghost found what it was looking for. Good-bye."

By four thirty my legal work was typed, filed, and I still had a job. The weekend never looked so good. I raced to my car, jumped in, and found myself stuck in the middle of Orange Avenue's stagnate traffic. Between traffic lights, I mentally meandered through Jack's frantic phone calls. My husband's ghost reports had raised a question worth pondering: was our specter really looking for something in that file cabinet, or was it just being obnoxious?

An hour later, I walked into my haunted house and headed straight for the study. In the far corner of the small room, the steel gray metal file cabinet faced me at military attention; every drawer was obediently closed except the last one. Something lay inside—something old and brown and withered. I picked it up.

The paperback, legal-sized notebook had seen the better part of this century and possibly part of the one before that. I was almost scared to touch it, lest it evaporate in a puff of sawdust. Its crumpling front and back jackets looked like they were made of recycled grocery bags; hundreds of onion skin pages lay between, secured at the top by two large brass clips. I peered closely at the neat, black typing across the front cover:

Abstract of Title

to

Certain Lands in Orange County, Florida

—

Central Title And

Trust Company

How had this gotten into my personal file cabinet? I knew every object that was stored in this old cabinet, except this mysterious book. I lifted the tattered bottom of the first page and scanned the faded description:

Description: All these certain lots…(*yadda, yadda*)… Lots 1 to 9 inclusive…(*blah, blah, blah*)…in Block "B"…(*whatever*)…of Smith's Woodlawn Addition…

Wait—this was the long-lost legal property record for this house!

I flipped to the next sheet. It was dated June 3, 1873, almost fifty-five years before my house was even built!

According to this first deed, Sam P. Hudson of Orange County, Florida, had bought my yard (or whatever it was at that time) for $1.25 an acre. Not a bad deal for swamp land.

The deeds and mortgages and affidavits and liens about my property droned on and on for the next five decades with still no mention of even a formal street name, much less construction. When exactly was my house built and who lived in it before my grandparents bought it in 1940? The greatest mystery of all was why these generations from practically every state in the Union kept buying a Florida bog, sight unseen? That was one question for which history had no logical answer.

After several dozen pages, an interesting document popped up: on August 7, 1926, a Eunice Wickham purchased the lot from Hill and James, Inc. Seven months and three mortgages later, a lease filed in Eunice's name on March 14, 1927, finally included the word *residence*. My house existed at last!

Sadly, the Wickhams became yet another casualty of Florida's frenzied building boom: ten months after the house was built, an improvement lien was filed against Eunice and her husband for $225.41. One month later, it had risen to $411.53. That was a lot of money to owe in 1929. Three liens and three mortgages accrued in two years: the Wickhams already had severe financial problems, with no idea that the bottom would drop out of the stock market by the end of the year.

I knew what was coming. With a gulp of impending doom, I forced myself to turn to the next page.

May 21, 1929: Stockton Mortgage Company filed the final foreclosure against the Wickhams. My mouth went dry. I stared at the yellowed paper which declared their residential death sentence. In less than two years, this family had built and lost their dream house. It seems a ghost wanted me to find this paper and know that my home's roots were sunk in despair.

The woman stood a stone's throw away on our front porch, a little to the left of the steps. Jack could have handed a rose to her, if there had been any to pick, but the elderly woman was distracted and didn't seem to notice him. The setting sun barely tinted her pale, lined face; such a gentle, sad face, looking just past Jack and deep into her own lost thoughts.

Her gray hair was piled into a practical bun on top of her head. The skirt of her plain beige house dress ended just above her ankles: a common-sense fashion which had been popular with housewives in the 1920s and '30s. Jack smiled; his own Italian great-grandmother had refused to give up the dresses or the native language of her youth. Every generation was allowed its own unique eccentricities. Happily, this somber woman wasn't totally devoid of style: Jack could see a faint lace pattern woven into the material of her garment. She was poor, but proud. Although Jack had never seen her before in his life, he knew who she was: Esther, the elderly missionary who had lived in our house with her husband and mother before we moved in.

Esther had politely plagued us with phone calls since the first day we reclaimed her former abode, and she always promised to drop by for a visit but never materialized. Jack stared at the motionless woman in front of him. Jack couldn't help feeling sorry for her. She looked so confused; even a little bewildered. Perhaps she was lonely.

"Hi, there." Jack waved happily at the woman.

She acted as if Jack wasn't there. Still silent, her fixed gaze looked past and through Jack at the same time. What was she looking for? More time? One more day in her beloved house that wasn't hers?

"Esther? Are you Esther? I'm Jack, Vivian's husband."

The woman disappeared. She didn't walk away. She never even moved. In front of Jack's unblinking eyes, the solid figure simply melted away. Only the whisper of the day's final sunbeam remained where she had stood.

It was somewhere around midnight and the dark-haired young woman stood in the black shadows of the upstairs hallway, watching Jack through the open door. Time was lost to Jack whenever he sat mesmerized in front of a computer game, but time was *always* lost to the woman.

Jack's neck began to ache. He'd been leaning over that keyboard for hours fighting aliens and wizards without a break. He turned his stiff head gently to the left.

Crick! That felt good. He turned his head to the right—and froze. In the midst of the shadows across from him scowled the woman. She radiated hatred. He wondered if this was the same bad-tempered ghost who had shoved me down the staircase five months ago. Never taking his eyes from the milky figure in the hall, Jack leaned out the doorway and yelled downstairs:

"Viv!"

The woman vanished. Jack practically flew down the stairs.

"It wasn't the sad old lady I saw yesterday," Jack panted in fright to me, "it was that witch who pushed you when you were unpacking the bedroom. She looks just like you described her: black hair, pale but pretty, about your height, but maybe a little younger than you. She was standing in the hallway, staring at me like she wanted to rip out my throat. I swear that I could feel hate spewing from her. What a viper!"

"Great," I sighed. "Now we have *two* ghosts!"

November 1993

"Hi! This is Uncle Ted! I hear I'm going to be a grand-father!"

His deep, jolly voice sounded like ground gravel, which may have been the result of long-distance back-ground static. The real mystery was why and how Uncle Ted was calling me in the first place: I was sound asleep, and he had been stone dead for almost a year.

Theodore W. Barns was Jack's step-grandfather, but he was known by one and all as Uncle Ted. I hadn't met the man in my life, but I knew him well from the many affectionate stories told by Jack and the rest of the Miller clan. Uncle Ted was Jersey City's fire chief, and he took advantage of his long lone hours in the fire station to study law. He passed the bar exam and, after retiring from the fire department, the self-taught attorney enjoyed a successful private practice for many years. He was as beloved by the community as he was by his family...and no one loved him more than Jack.

"Uncle Ted used to take me out to eat at the Windmill, which was a local hamburger joint in Longbranch, New Jersey. They had the best burgers for miles around! We'd sit by the beach and watch the seagulls swoop and steal our fries against the sunset. Then we'd drive back to his place and stay up all night watching *No Time for Sergeants* on TV. Every time that I see that movie, I like to think that Uncle Ted is watching it over my shoulder and laughing his head off."

Uncle Ted's last words were about his adopted grandson: "Even though he wasn't part of my blood, I've always thought of Jack as my own." Jack missed his Uncle Ted as much as Uncle Ted apparently missed him!

Several months after his death, on a cold and rainy December night in Florida, Uncle Ted called in my dreams. Baby Erin wasn't due to arrive for another three months, but I was already exhausted. So far I'd endured all the usual side-effects of pregnancy, but receiving psychic phone messages from dead in-laws was a new one to me!

Uncle Ted interrupted a wonderful dream that I never quite recalled. Right in the middle of the most exciting part, everything went pitch black, darker than dark—like a TV screen cut off during a blackout. After a second of silence, out of the void came a friendly, rough voice that sounded as if it was on the other end of a long-distance phone call. *Very* long distance, as it turned out.

"Hi! This is Uncle Ted! I hear I'm going to be a grandfather!" Suddenly, he stopped short and began arguing with someone in the blackness. "No! Wait! I'm not done yet…." His voice was suddenly cut off in the middle of his next word, as if his end of the phone had been abruptly hung up. My original dream popped back in full color, exactly in the spot at which it had been interrupted. I was clearly aware that I was asleep during all this and I meant to tell Jack about Uncle Ted's message, just as soon as I figured out how to wake myself up.

But like most dreams, my memory of Uncle Ted's call faded with the sunrise. I had no recollection of it until several days later, right in the middle of dinner:

"Oh, yeah! Jack, I forgot to tell you about this really weird dream that I had a couple of nights ago. At least, I think it was a dream. It felt different, almost like it was real."

Jack chewed his spaghetti. By the time I'd finished my short story, he was about to choke.

"Describe the voice to me," he whispered.

"Well, let's see," I mused. "It was deep and kind of scratchy. But it was very, very kind, not gruff at all. It sounded like a grandfather's voice should sound, you know?"

Jack's face drained of color. "That's exactly how Uncle Ted sounded. I couldn't have described it better myself! I'm going to give my mother a call."

"Oh, please don't do that!" I begged. "She'll think I'm a nut." During our two years of marriage, I'd only met one of Jack's sisters in person; the rest of his family lived miles away in New York and New Jersey, and face-to-face introductions were expensive in those days; none of us had the extra money for air fare. Our phone conversations were civil and limited to rational, non-ghostly subjects. Jack's mom was planning to fly down to Orlando in March to welcome her fourth grandchild; how could I face her after she heard about my wacky dream? Before I had a chance to really form my argument, Jack had already dialed his mother.

"Mom talked with Gram," Jack reported. Gram was Jack's maternal grandmother and Uncle Ted's loving widow. "They both agree that was Uncle Ted's voice. Gram was so relieved to know that he's doing well and is happy on the Other Side that she burst into tears of joy." Jack was grinning from ear to ear. "To tell you the truth, I'm happy, too."

"But, why did he talk to *me?*" I argued. "Not only am I not really related to him, but I never met the man, spoke to him, or saw his photo in my life. I'd think that he would prefer to talk with you or Gram."

"Except that Gram and I aren't carrying his grandchild," Jack replied.

Good point. Who knows? Maybe unborn Baby Erin could somehow plug into her mommy's dreams for a three-way phone call. Maybe this was the most direct way that Uncle Ted could welcome his newest great-grandchild. Love transcends all boundaries, from the afterlife to life-to-be and everywhere in between. Uncle Ted gave me the best baby present of all!

December 24, 1993

I stared across the front room at my reflection. I had never looked so pale. My face was milky and the hem of my long white nightgown covered my feet. And what happened to my seven-months-pregnant bloated stomach? It now looked as svelte as Barbie in a bikini! Oddest of all, I was mirrored on the plaster wall beside the fireplace. Since when did chalky, flaking plaster act like a mirror? No, that wasn't right. I wasn't reflected *on* the wall—the mirror image of my body was standing several feet in front of it.

Ghosts always seem to pop up when you least expect them.

Unable to sleep that Christmas Eve, I had wandered into the shadowy front room to check on our new little dog, Abby, who was sleeping. As I knelt beside Abby's bed under the archway between the dining room and the front room, I felt as if I was being watched. I glanced up to find myself staring at a girl across the room; a girl so real that I assumed it was my own reflection, mirrored on the far wall somehow by the ceiling light shining from the dining room behind me. Science has never been my strong point.

"Too weird!" I muttered to myself. I gave snoring Abby a final pat on her fuzzy white head and stood up to return to my own bedroom. My "reflection" didn't move an inch. I turned to leave, then took a last peek over my shoulder. The figure was now standing several feet closer to me than it had been only a moment before!

It had to be a trick of the light. Never taking my eyes off the misty form, I reached over to the wall switch and slowly turned the dining room light off and on. The girl was a bit fainter under the bright light, but she was still plainly visible. I turned the light off again. Still staring at me. Light on. Girl there. Light off. Girl still there. The only thing I was accomplishing was wearing out the toggle switch.

Curious, confused, and still certain that I was witnessing a strange reflection of myself, I leaned against the archway, crossed my arms, and took a good, long look. The girl appeared to be in her early twenties (a decade younger than I) and was about my height of five-six, maybe a bit shorter. Her cloudy face was indistinct but clearly attractive. She reminded me of a monochromatic Monet watercolor. Her long, flowing white dress began with a gently curved neckline that was gathered by a silky ribbon; the long sleeves billowed and pleated at her wrists like Juliet's balcony nightgown. Light brown hair fell to her shoulders, thick and straight except for a full under-curl at the ends.

Shoulder-length hair? Wait a minute. Mine had been cut into a short bob last week! And my graceful attire was a thick terrycloth robe with bunchy sleeves and a droopy sash. Strangest of all, my "reflection" surveyed me with equal puzzlement and surprise, as if I was the intruder! There was no animosity between us—we just couldn't figure out how on earth that other person was suddenly standing in our dark living room. It was time to harness a third-party opinion to solve this mystery. As I walked back into the bedroom for a discussion with Jack, I could feel my "reflection" watching my every step. The house was silent except for Abby, who continued to snore like a freight train.

Jack had apparently given up on sleep that night, too; I found him sitting up in bed, happily engrossed in a thick book.

"I just saw the weirdest thing!" I began. "I thought that I saw my reflection beside the fireplace, but that didn't make sense because …" By the end of my tale, Jack's eyes were wider than the full moon.

"I'm going out there to have a look," my husband announced, rolling out of bed.

"Why? Whatever it is, it's probably gone by now." Wouldn't it be just typical for my fickle phantom to vanish without waiting for a witness?

"Except for the white nightgown, you just described exactly the same girl that I've been seeing in the upstairs hallway."

I considered his comparison. "The problem is that the girl that I just saw was anything but angry. She wasn't rushing over to shake hands with me, but she certainly wasn't going to slam me against the wall, either. I don't think she'd ever seen me before."

"Or maybe she didn't remember you," Jack added. He walked into the dark front room, closing our bedroom door behind him.

He was back in a flash.

"Did you see her?"

"Not exactly." Jack tried to act as if his entire body wasn't shaking like the San Andreas fault. "I saw a weird pillar of light, almost like an electric fire, glowing in the same spot that you described seeing the girl. It was fading when I spotted it and disappeared completely a few seconds later. If the room hadn't been so dark, I probably wouldn't have noticed it at all."

I sighed. "And I thought only Santa showed up on Christmas Eve!"

January 1994

The pounding footsteps shook our entire house. Rivaling our doors' performance from the previous spring, these invisible footfalls clumped noisily up and down the stairs and into the upstairs hallway as the spirit moved them. They had bumped through Thanksgiving dinner, pounded over our Christmas celebration, and thumped in the New Year with us. Just like the slamming doors, they never, ever made a peep if anyone was in the house other than Jack or me.

They were even on their best behavior during Ian's visits.

My patience with this latest paranormal prank finally wore out one January afternoon when they almost walked in on me in the upstairs bathroom. Jack was out, so I decided to pamper myself with a well-deserved hot bubble bath in the middle of the day. I had to take full advantage of the next few weeks; my due date was on the horizon and after that, the only person in this house who would be using a bottle of Mr. Bubble would be Baby Erin.

In the middle of my soak, the pesky footsteps decided to pay a visit. As always, the din began abruptly at the foot of the stairway on the ground floor and then slowly dragged themselves up each step: BOOM! BOOM! BOOM!

"Must they always stomp?" I fumed to myself from my warm tub.

CLUMP! They reached the upstairs hallway. BUMP! BUMP! They slowly made their way down the passage, then stopped short in front of my closed bathroom door. Who, living or otherwise, would have the audacity to interrupt an expectant mother trying to relax in a much needed bubble bath?

"Do you mind?" I bellowed from my tub. "I'd like a little privacy!"

The footsteps promptly clomped across the hall into Ian's large bedroom. They sounded almost embarrassed. I had the feeling that this noisy wraith was a man, since the stair-pushing witch would have tried to drown me. Our household ghost count was now up to three: the old woman, the shoving witch, and now the stair-clomping man. There was only one logical thing to do: I phoned my mother.

"You grew up in this house, Mama. Did you ever hear footsteps like these? Especially by the upstairs bathroom? Especially when you were *in* the upstairs bathroom?"

"Well, dear, you grew up in that house too, you know." she replied. "I remember lying in my bed at night as a child and listening to the stairs creaking long after my parents were asleep. My mother always insisted that I sleep with the light off, and I'm sure that I thought that I heard all sorts of strange noises in the middle of the night. When I mentioned those sounds to Mother, she explained it was only the wooden steps expanding with the rising heat from that big gas furnace in the front room downstairs. You know what? Mother was right! I would hear that heater click on and then those old stairs would start to slowly groan, one by one, exactly as if someone was walking up them. After that, those little noises never bothered me a bit."

"Jack and I threw that old heater out months ago. We only have a couple of little space heaters in our bedroom downstairs, and those are barely enough to warm our bed. These footsteps stomp all over the house, whether our little electric heaters are on or not."

"Well, maybe the house is just saying hello to you," my mother replied.

I sighed.

"If it makes you feel any better," my mother continued, "Aunt Grace once told me that she thought the house was haunted."

I almost fell out of my chair! "Aunt Grace said *what*? You never told me that!" There was not a more reputable witness on the face of the earth than ancient Aunt Grace. A close friend of my grandparents, she had been a Baptist missionary and a profound Christian all of her life; to even imagine her uttering the word *ghost* would be blasphemous.

"Don't underestimate Aunt Grace," warned Mama. "You only knew her as a sweet little old lady. She was a smart, tough woman and knew exactly what she was talking about. During her missionary days, she worked with some very primitive tribes in the jungles of South America and even knew some witch doctors who warned her about the reality of evil spirits in our world."

"So what did she tell you about our house?" I persisted.

"It happened while she and her family were living in our house. You remember that Granddaddy allowed her to stay there, rent free, since she was elderly and in ill health? Well, one afternoon, she and I were visiting together in the front room, waiting for Esther, her equally elderly daughter, to bring us some tea. We were having a lovely conversation, when she suddenly leaned over to me and whispered, 'This place has spooks, you know!' Well, I was dumbfounded! I just sat there with my mouth open, not a clue how to respond to her.

"'Sometimes they walk into my room at night, but I don't say anything about it', Aunt Grace persisted. 'Believe me, this house is haunted!'

"But Esther laughed as she came back in with her mother's tea. 'Oh, Mother, you're just being silly!' Grace took a little sip, smiled knowingly and said, 'Oh, I don't know about that...' She never said another word about it again.

"I never took Aunt Grace seriously," my mother concluded. "I thought she was just going a bit senile until your stories started. Now, I'm not sure."

Actually, Aunt Grace wasn't the first person I knew to accuse my house of being haunted. Fourteen years ago, one of my college roommates, Samantha, spent a Thanksgiving break here that she would never forget ...

November 1979

What was old Esther doing in Samantha's room watching her sleep?

The cool darkness had finally brought blessed sleep to Sam's pounding migraine. For three straight hours she had battled the pain until she collapsed, defeated, on my antique bed with every light switched off on the second floor of our house. She and I had escaped from our college in West Palm Beach to spend Thanksgiving break with my grandfather in Orlando. Since his tiny apartment sported only a single sleeper sofa for guests, we happily opted to stay at his house—our house—with his good friend Aunt Grace, her daughter Esther, and Esther's husband Leonard. Atheist Sam's initial response to living with a bunch of missionaries was on par with being asked to drink strychnine. Her agreement came with the stark realization that spending a holiday stuck on a deserted college campus fell way below the missionary problem.

Sam had begun Thanksgiving Day with only a whisper of a headache, but by that evening it had turned into Hurricane Migraine: candlelight blinded her, the sound of a pin drop sent screaming waves of pain through her tender skull, the touch of a fingertip to her temple felt

like a cannonball smashing her head. When my grandfather invited us to go to the movies with him, Sam politely
declined—hours held captive in front of a large luminous
screen would cause her head to explode. Granddaddy and
I went to the movie theatre, and Sam went to bed.

Seconds or hours later (she couldn't tell which), a
beam from the full moon crept through my bedroom
window and kissed Sam's closed eyes softly. She groaned.
Her head was finally calm, but her body craved sleep.
What time was it, anyway? Sam opened her eyes to peek
at the bedside clock. She saw the woman instead.

Moonlight danced off her gray hair, which was neatly
caught up in a bun on top of her head. She sat comfortably in my great-grandmother Jenny Andre's rocker,
gently swaying to and fro. Although her face was turned
away from Sam and toward the open window, there was
no doubt in Sam's mind who it was: there were only two
old ladies in this house and it sure wasn't crippled Aunt
Grace in her wheelchair. It had to be her elderly daughter,
Esther. Obviously the kind old missionary had decided to
stay by her ailing guest's side, but Sam felt no comfort;
this lady gave her the creeps! Outraged that her privacy
had been invaded, grumpy Sam sat straight up in bed and
snarled at the rude figure, "What are you doing in here?"

The woman stopped rocking. Slowly, she turned her
head toward Sam.

It was a face that Sam had never seen before.

The horrified girl grasped frantically for the pull chain on the old glass bedside lamp, but in her haste, she sent the light crashing to the floor instead. Leaping out of bed, she fumbled across the dark bedroom and groped for the wall light switch. The woman remained still in the rocker; only her head turned as she silently followed Sam's every move with her wide, unblinking eyes.

Sam switched on the ceiling light. The empty wooden rocker continued to sway back and forth, back and forth, back and forth …

Sam tore down the staircase and into the living room where Esther and her family were gathered, quietly sharing their evening devotions.

"Goodness, Samantha!" The old woman exclaimed in the middle of reciting her tenth Bible verse, "What's wrong?"

Sam raced to Esther, collapsed in her arms, and took a long look at her very compassionate, very alive face. No, she definitely was not the woman in the rocker.

"Could I stay down here with you?" Sam whimpered in a small voice.

Praise the Lord! The missionaries were overjoyed to have Sam as a temporary member of their gathering.

Thirty minutes later, I returned home from my date with my granddad. No sooner had I unlocked the front door than Sam raced across the room and embraced me like an eager child.

"Vivian! You're home! What took you so long?"

"Sam, let me go!" I gasped as my friend knocked me head over heels. "You've got me locked in a vise."

Sam released my neck, grabbed my arm, and dragged me up the stairs.

"What the heck is wrong with you?" I demanded as soon as my bedroom door was shut soundly behind us. "You were *praying* with the missionaries."

Samantha looked me straight in the eye. "This house is haunted!"

I may have had some spooky adventures, but this wasn't like practical Sam at all. "What exactly did you take for that headache?"

Sam was serious. Her story shot out so fast that my ears could barely keep up. Had this been told by anyone else I may have had my doubts, but Samantha was the most logical, fact-based, show-me-the-solid-evidence person I'd ever met. Her firm disbelief in any type of god was only the beginning of her skepticism, ghosts being so far "out there" that she wouldn't even waste her time smirking at a Casper cartoon. She also had to be fully awake in order to cross the dark bedroom without falling over several pieces of furniture, and I knew first-hand that my roommate wasn't a sleepwalker, so that ruled out a nightmare.

I walked over to the rocker, which originally belonged to my grandfather's French mother, Jenny Andre. Sam's description of the ghost sounded a lot like the old family photos I'd seen of her. Gray hair piled on top of her head…long dress…I moved my hand across the rocker. "The seat's warm."

"That does it!" Samantha exclaimed. "I am not sleeping in here tonight and I'm not going to let you either."

"Sam, that's silly," I retorted. "I slept in this room when I was a kid and whenever we visited Granddaddy, and I've always been fine. I'll admit that sometimes I thought that I saw weird stuff—"

Knock knock.

Someone, or something, was tapping on my closed bedroom door. We eyed the swaying rocker.

"Don't you *dare* open it!" my roommate hissed.

Knock knock knock.

The glass doorknob began to turn by itself as my door swung open. In the hallway stood the dark form of a woman with gray hair.

"Well, hello there, girls!" Esther beamed. "Would you care to come back downstairs and join us for the rest of our Bible study?"

Spring 1994

Jack was thirsty. All he wanted to do was grab a Coke from the fridge. The problem was how to walk around that enormous black…shadow…*thing* that had stretched across the entire kitchen doorway. Long, spindly legs shuddered and sprawled out at insane angles from its craggy, bloated body. It looked like a demonic spider. No eyes; no face. Only legs. Lots and lots of legs.

"I'm going into the kitchen and nothing is going to stop me!" Jack announced aloud with all the determination of a fox escaping a hellhound. The Spider Shadow didn't buy Jack's bravado; it remained solidly in place, slowly weaving back and forth in silent mockery, daring that insipid human to pass.

It was Jack's turn again. Like a man who would be king, he marched straight toward the monster Spider Shadow. *Move fast. Don't breathe. Don't stop.*

One step.

The creature didn't budge.

Two steps.

Still there.

Jack's determined pace never slowed. He was a locomotive ready to rake the cow off the track, no matter the consequence.

Three steps. Four…

The Spider Shadow suddenly lurched upward, stretching above the doorway to its full height for a long moment before springing straight up and clinging upside-down to the paint-scarred ceiling just as Jack strode underneath it. Jack's legs were wet sponges as he slid under the demonic form and smashed into the front of the refrigerator. Would he have been able to scream if that thing had wrapped all those stringy cockroach legs around his throat? Would his eyeballs have popped, then shriveled like a slug covered in salt? Hell's spider was still hanging like a bat right outside the kitchen doorway. The longer Jack stared at the inverted black bug, the more the kitchen sink began to look like a comfortable place to spend the night. He popped open a cold can of Coke and considered his future ...

Three minutes after midnight on March 14, 1994, Erin Campbell-Miller bounced into the world. My life-long dream had come true: I had a daughter!

Most parents can hardly wait to carry their darling new offspring to their home, but we dreaded leaving the hospital. I'm told that on the day that my parents first carried me across our threshold, our sunlit house was filled with bouquets of flowers, pink and yellow fuzzy baby toys, and two grandparents beaming with pride. Everything radiated love and joy. Thirty-two years later, I arrived on that same doorstep with my own baby girl. I carried her inside, unstrapped her from her baby carrier, and placed the seat carefully in a corner by the bedroom door. Five minutes later, I glanced up from the changing table where I was struggling with Erin's tiny diaper ... and froze at the sight before me.

"Jack, did you move the baby carrier?"

"No, I haven't touched it," Jack called from the other side of the bathroom door. "Why?"

In the center of the room lay Erin's baby carrier, upside-down and backward, sprawled like the body of a battered child that had been viciously and silently kicked to death.

The next morning, Jack decided to escape to his office two hours earlier than usual, leaving three-day-old Erin and me alone together in the house for the first time since her birth. The night had been unnervingly quiet. Erin's thrown baby carrier was a pointed warning that I chose to ignore but not to forget. Instead, I immersed myself in something far more important: enjoying my baby! Erin and I were finally free from the constant interruption of hospital doctors and nurses waking us up at all hours to make sure we were still breathing. Our first morning together at home dawned sunny, warm, and clear; the whole world beamed with another new life. The transformed house seemed wrapped around us like a big satin comforter. The air sparkled as sunlight skipped up and down the stairs. Best of all, for the first time in ninety-five years, Great-Grandma Jenny's rocker once again gently lulled a newborn member of our family in its lap.

My friend Tammy had kindly offered to drop by later that morning to watch over Erin as she napped so I could catch a nap as well. Since Tammy wasn't certain of her arrival time, I told her to just let herself in with our hidden extra house key, so as not to risk waking my baby with a ringing doorbell. I left my bedroom door ajar and positioned the rocker where I could sit undisturbed with Erin and still clearly see Tammy when she walked in the front door.

The old rocker worked its enchantment and Erin slumbered in my lap. All morning I gazed at the face of my sleeping baby girl. She was a miracle beyond magic. I didn't even bother to glance up when I heard the soft, solid footsteps crossing our living room. *Funny, I didn't hear the front door open*, I thought to myself. Never taking my eyes off Erin, I softly called out, "Hey, Tammy—we're in here."

Silence.

"Tammy?"

Step.

Step.

Step.

"Jack?"

Only the rhythm of two feet treading slowly around the front room answered me. From the sound of it, Tammy must have been stomping. *That's weird*. I leaned forward from my rocker to get a better peek out of my partly opened bedroom door. There wasn't a living soul in sight. I was thankful that at least this time the house had the courtesy not to shake like an earthquake. This tread was different than the ones I had heard on the stairs and in the upstairs hall; these footfalls were deliberate, like a businessman inspecting the surroundings of his future office. As soon as my eyes scanned the outer room, the steps suddenly stopped, turned, and then crossed straight toward me over the hardwood floor and century-old carpets. I was too amazed to even blink. I simply sat in Jenny's rocker with my sleeping child held close to my heart, straining my eyes to see the source of the sound that distinctly walked closer and closer across the sunlit rooms. We had been discovered.

The footsteps paused at my doorway. The house held its breath for a blink, then my partly opened door swung open to its full width. Nothing stood before us, but I felt it gaze down with a "Gotcha!" sneer. Never moving from my rocker and balancing my sleeping baby, I stuck out my right foot and kicked the door shut in the face of whatever was there.

"Don't mess with my baby!" I angrily muttered through gritted teeth at the closed door. "You won't win. I'll make sure of it."

Margaret Miller, my visiting mother-in-law, stared at the old woman standing at the foot of her bed. Although the light had just been turned out for the night, the woman was as visible and as solid as the house's white plaster walls. Her long black dress was old-fashioned but stylish, with lovely puffy mutton sleeves and a quaint bustle in the back. Margaret was certain that was a bustle; she could see it clearly reflected in the full-length mirror behind the woman. The lovely gray hair was pulled up in a sensible bun on top of her head and adorned with a black lace Spanish mantilla headpiece that fell down the back of her neck.

Obviously this stranger was another visiting relative to whom she had not yet been introduced. Perhaps she was a very eccentric great-great aunt who had toddled by unexpectedly to admire the baby. Her large, sad eyes looked lost. It was almost one in the morning; maybe the tired old woman had mixed up her assigned bedroom with the one that Margaret had already been given. Margaret had only arrived in Orlando a few hours ago to visit her three-week-old granddaughter for the first time, so she had no idea what our baby viewing schedule was, nor did she really care. She had only two main goals right now: cuddling her precious little Erin and helping out Erin's exhausted mommy and daddy.

As Margaret sat alone in the middle of the big antique bed gazing back at the old woman, a second pair of eyes bored into her. Glancing to her left, Margaret spotted a second woman, much younger than the first, standing silently on the other side of her bed. Margaret peered at her closed bedroom door. The latch was fixed tight.

Never moving from her fixed spot in bed, Margaret inspected the younger woman more closely. Her ash-blond hair fell gracefully a little below the shoulders of her floor-length white nightgown. The garment flowed with long billowy sleeves and a scooped neckline that had a ribbon laced gracefully through it. Her young features appeared to be pretty but were difficult to distinguish because, in the darkness of the room, her face appeared to be almost translucent. In fact, Margaret swore she could actually see the rear wall right through the young woman's entire body!

Then Margaret Miller knew she wasn't the victim of wandering houseguests; she was surrounded by two ghosts.

Fear was no deterrent. Through no want of her own, spirits had been attracted to Margaret since the day she took her first step. It was a family trait. She was a pro and knew just what to do in this situation. Grabbing the rosary she had carefully hung on the bedpost by her pillow, she closed her eyes:

"Holy Virgin, spread your protective white light over me and over all of my loved ones in this house. Send our guardian angels to drive out these unwanted spirits." Margaret opened her eyes. The ghosts were gone. She could breathe again. Somewhere, the clock struck two.

"Son, did you know that there are two ghosts in your house?"

Jack's cereal spoon froze halfway to his open mouth. His mother politely contemplated her morning coffee as she paused to give her son time to either finish his corn flakes or answer her question.

Jack cleared his throat nervously. "Um, actually we've known about them for a while." His mother's comment didn't entirely surprise him. Margaret Miller's psychic abilities were famous throughout her immediate family, although no one had ever mentioned this fact to me, her fairly new daughter-in-law. It was a family secret passed down in guarded whispers rather than public announcements.

Margaret had reportedly inherited her gift from her Irish mother, Tracy. Tracy's Swedish stepmother taught her how to foretell the future by reading coffee grounds. Tracy's talent proved to be quite accurate and she enjoyed predicting for many years until one day she casually looked into her coffee cup and was horrified to read that her best friend would die in either "three years, three months, or three days." Terrified, she kept the deadly prophecy to herself and fervently prayed that it was wrong. Three days later, that same dear friend was killed due to carbon monoxide poisoning. Tracy refused to ever read another coffee ground for the rest of her ninety-eight years.

Apparently Margaret was so sensitive to spirits that she could stand in the middle of a street and warn, "That blue house on the left is haunted. I wouldn't go in there if I were you. The spirits there are angry and may cause trouble." Although Margaret took her ability seriously, she was a devout Roman Catholic and avoided drawing attention to her gift unless she felt that someone's safety was at risk. Even then, she would try to explain her sudden dizzy spells or loss of breath as "just a head cold" or some other socially acceptable condition. She was a gentle, loving, giving woman who was content to let her children tease her. She would rather die than scare them, but she would rather scare them than allow any evil spirit to infiltrate her family.

"Mom, I think you'd better discuss this problem with Vivian after she wakes up," Jack continued. "I'm late for work."

Margaret poured herself a second cup of coffee and patiently waited for me to rouse myself after another sleepless night with my newborn. Thirty minutes later her coffee had done nothing to deter her yawns; she decided to return upstairs for a short nap in the big antique bed.

Ah yes! The bed! It was a century older than our haunted house, with memories enough, surely. It was elegant and extraordinary, with hand-carved roses adorning both sides of its massive rosewood foot, side, and headboards. It was created before the Civil War and given as a gift to my grandmother Mary in the early 1950s by one of her dear friends, a charming elderly widow named Mrs. Starbuck. The magical bed had been in Mrs. Starbuck's family for so many years that not even ancient Mrs. Starbuck could remember exactly how old it was; decades later, several antique appraisers assured me that it was created no earlier than 1860.

My Scottish great-grandfather, William Hosie, was the first member of our family to fall asleep in the bed's massive arms. He liked it so much that he even died in it. Thirteen years later, I announced that it would be my bed, though at the time I was barely old enough to crawl out of my crib that lay beside it. From that day, the bed—*my* bed—never failed to protect me from monsters in the night, both imagined and real, as my books and I snuggled under a cascading lavender satin comforter during my frequent all-night reading binges, both as a young child and during my numerous visits. It was on this safe, serene bed that my mother-in-law had spent a sleepless night and now stretched out for a much-deserved nap.

Mid-morning sunbeams danced through the closed bedroom drapes. Margaret didn't care. Those two pesky ghosts had kept her up almost all night, making her much too tired to let a little daylight keep her awake. With a yawn, she lay down in my warm old bed, turned over comfortably on her left side, and pulled the thick cover over her shoulders.

Then something touched her beneath the bedcovers. Something dark and evil, that pressed fully against the entire length of her right side like a grinning Hannibal-the-Cannibal Lecter, ready to take a big bite out of her back. With a start, Margaret began to roll over to face her assailant, but her body refused to cooperate. She couldn't so much as budge her big toe. She was paralyzed from head to foot by a malevolence that wrapped unseen appendages around her ribs and crushed itself against her back. The cowardly thing wouldn't even look her in the face.

Margaret's brain screamed for a logical answer. She knew it was a medical fact that during a certain stage of sleep, the human body becomes paralyzed. The problem was that Margaret hadn't had time to even close her eyes. No, she was fully awake, squinting against the bright daylight that flooded her bed prison. The thing still lay against her prone body, squeezing, squeezing...

Gasping, Margaret tried to call out for help, but even her voice was stilled. She was nothing more than a helpless captive forced to lay against a leering phantom that panted against the base of her neck. Margaret refused to give up. She struggled. She fought with every drop of adrenaline she could muster. After what seemed like a lifetime, she managed to lift her right arm up far enough to touch the nearest bedpost and her fingers brushed against her beloved rosary, still hanging in its place from the night before. Her strength ended there. She was too weak, too exhausted, to lift the chain over to her heart. Hanging on to the holy object, her only lifeline, Margaret Miller prayed and prayed and prayed.

Weariness finally overtook her. By some miracle, she slipped into sleep—a blessed, deep, dreamless sleep that renewed her body and soul. She awoke with the same sunbeams dancing around the room, but the evil presence was gone. Margaret Miller, brave and faithful far beyond human strength, was free.

"Well, Erin's finally asleep and I'm conscious. Sort of." I groggily dragged myself out of my bedroom and stumbled into the breakfast nook. My uncombed hair probably looked like it had been styled by a lightning bolt; my puffy red eyes rolled like half-chewed gumballs and I tripped over the hem of my trusty-but-dusty terrycloth robe. I peered at the kitchen wall clock. It was past noon. What a way to begin the first morning alone with my mother-in-law.

Margaret Miller handed me a fresh cup of steaming coffee. The dark circles under her eyes spoke a thousand words.

"How was your night? I hope Erin didn't keep you awake," I ventured.

"No, no, *she* didn't keep me awake," Margaret pointedly answered.

"Don't tell me those lousy neighbors in that old duplex kept you up!" I angrily exclaimed. "I've had to phone the police about them three times since we moved here. The next time I see the owner of that ugly little building, I'm going to warn him to find some renters who are at least law-abiding, or I'll call the cops on him too! I can't apologize enough…"

"Vivian, the neighborhood was quiet all night."

I gave her a puzzled look. "Was it that old bed, then? That's a brand-new mattress on it, but if it's too hard for you I'll be glad to…"

Margaret placed her hand reassuringly over mine. "Vivian, please don't worry. It's nothing that you've done. We need to have a talk."

"A talk?" I gulped.

"About your ghosts." She smiled. Oh, no. After all these years of only picking on Jack and myself, had our eccentric phantoms suddenly decided to plague my poor mother-in-law, as well?

"Why?" I gulped again.

"Because you have to protect my granddaughter, no matter what."

January 1995

Jack waved at the woman that stared at him through our dining room window.

"Hey, Viv! It's okay. I'm still alive out here—just wanted to get this lawn mowed." Jack's friendly greeting was returned with an icy stare. Wondering at "my" dour expression, Jack peered closer. The woman was vaguely familiar, but she certainly wasn't me! Her dark hair was piled on top of her head in an old-fashioned Victorian style; she was at least two generations ahead of me and looked nine times as mean.

Old Mrs. Brown from down the street must have dropped in to see the baby, Jack mused to himself. Odd. Mrs. Brown was never without a smile; this matron looked like she licked lemons.

I know I've seen her before but, where? Funny, I didn't notice her come up the front walkway. I didn't even hear the front door open. Why would a neighbor stand in a dark room by herself?

Jack brushed away the grass and leaves from his pants leg and marched up the front porch steps to greet the mysterious matron. The dark, empty house greeted him with silence.

"Hello? Viv?" Jack closed the front door behind him and nervously cleared his throat. "Is anybody home?" Only the dripping kitchen faucet answered. Jack switched on the lights and peered around the corner into the adjoining library where he had just seen the disapproving woman. The empty room peered back.

A soft glow caught Jack's eye. Baby Erin's night light was shining under the closed door to our bedroom. Jack cracked the door open and looked in. A shadowed female form sat in the old rocking chair. She held something in her lap.

"Vivian," he whispered, "Have you and Erin been in here for the last ten minutes or so?"

I awoke with a start and looked up from the rocker where my baby and I sat snoozing.

Jack's pale expression left no doubt for the real reason behind his question.

"Which ghost did you see this time, the old lady or that hateful young woman?" I yawned. Our spooks were getting tiresome.

"I think it was the old lady," Jack decided. "Her hair was up in that high bun, but this time the color looked dark, not gray. No, it had to be the old lady, because the younger woman's hair usually hangs loose around her shoulders. Why would an old lady ghost watch me work in the yard?"

"Because she's an old snoop!" I loudly snapped back in frustration. My condemnation was plainly aimed at whatever might be eavesdropping in the dense darkness surrounding us. "Why couldn't we just have termites like normal people? What are we supposed to do to get rid of *these* pests? Call a Ghostbuster?"

Jack replied with a tense chuckle, walked out of the room, and turned on every single light in the entire house, electric bill be damned.

I rocked sleeping Erin on my lap, but internally I was steaming mad at our snoopy spooks. My house had been so quiet for so long. Barely a shadow had waved at us for months; we had been lulled into a false sense of security. Three months of living in a "normal" house had again blown up in our faces. The ghostly pranks that started as quirky subjects to chuckle over had mutated into vicious attacks determined to drive us out of "their" house. Just like the rude old woman that Jack spotted at the window tonight, we could feel them silently sneer at us, *What are you still doing here?*

My patience was gone. Whose family lived in this house since 1940? Not that old lady's with the bad hair! I didn't care who built this house; we'd had legal ownership for a half-century. I had a baby to protect and a house to reclaim.

"War is declared!" I snarled to the surrounding darkness.

The next morning, the glass cabinet doors on my grandmother's massive antique secretary began unlocking and opening by themselves. My proclamation had been heard and answered.

Jack walked slowly through our house, which was darker than usual except for an eerie glow. Out of the iridescent gloom, the old woman appeared in front of him. Determined not to be deterred, Jack struggled to take another step forward, but the ancient matron refused to move out of his way. She stared placidly at him.

"You have to leave this house!" Jack admonished the genteel hag.

The old woman's shriveled voice floated through the gloom. "But, you don't understand!"

She sounded like a frustrated grandmother admonishing a stubborn child.

"You *have* to leave this house!" Jack repeated.

"You don't understand. You don't understand."

Their conversation repeated itself over and over, neither one convincing the other or offering to move.

Jack sat up in bed, his body slimed with raw, icy sweat. "I've just had a waking dream!" he gasped beside me in the dark.

"What do you mean by a 'waking dream'?" I muttered into my pillow.

"It was the old woman. She said—"

"The ghost? She *spoke*?" Now I was wide awake. "What did she say?"

Jack gulped. "I think it was a warning."

May 17, 1995

The black mist snaked its way silently down the stairs, pausing only to curl seductively around the ground floor banister. For the past six months it had lain dormant, only slithering down and around long after midnight to assess its opportunities in the unsuspecting stillness of the night. From its perch, it could see the pale electric light glowing from the room below. That's where the child was.

The clock struck four a.m. as another endless episode of *Little House on the Prairie* popped on the TV screen. Baby Erin had managed to switch her nights and days, so she merrily bounced and swayed in her infant swing beside the front room couch where I lay, hypnotized by Ma and Pa Ingalls through red-rimmed sleep-deprived eyes. My head hurt. My back ached. My hands stank of diaper cream. Goosebumps and ghosts were the last thing I needed, but that was exactly what I got. I glanced away from Walnut Grove just in time to spy the curling tube of black fog seep down the last stair step and steer its murky head toward us. It was an anaconda with teeth, disguised under a mask of dark mist. I grabbed Erin out of her swing, dashed into our bedroom, and left the snarling mist alone with the televised Ingalls family. At least Pa had a pitchfork.

The spectral serpent fog continued its nightly visits. Erin and I were stalked almost every evening that we sat alone together in the wee hours, with or without the Ingalls family. The mist would allow us a night or two of freedom, then the smoky viper would curl into the room and I would beat a hasty retreat, waving my coward's white flag with Erin in tow. I refused to fight such a thing with my infant daughter. Escape was easy: we simply shut the bedroom door behind us. The mist would swirl around the front room for an hour or so, sniffing and searching, then return up the stairway and melt into the second floor's darkness to wait for the next evening's hunt. Despite my efforts to restore the upstairs master bedroom, the nightly phantom fog had deterred our moving anyone, including Erin's crib and baby furniture, out of our original downstairs bedroom. We had been cowering in that "safe" room since the day we moved into the house. But I knew I would have to end this constant retreat soon and confront the phantoms once and for all.

The ensuing paranormal battle began late one evening as I sat alone in the front room. Erin, my usual late-night chum, was miraculously snoring away in her crib behind the closed bedroom door, but my nerves were twisted like an overwound clock. Armed with a thick book, I settled into the large comfy lap of our living room couch and relaxed in lost memories of my childhood. Rare moments like this with my beloved Jekyll-and-Hyde house were pure treasure. This old building was the only part of my family that would never die as long as it was in my care. As much trouble as the house gave us, it also gave us great joy.

Grandma's clock bonged twice. A slight breeze flipped a page in my book. I glanced up. All of the windows around me were shut tight and central air conditioning was absent in our 1927 house. Another icy breath bit into my face. I looked toward the stairway. The fog twisted around the last banister like a holiday wreath for a Black Mass.

Without demonstrated hurry, I closed my book, rose from my seat, and wandered into the kitchen for a glass of water. Since the meddlesome mist never drifted farther than the front room, I logically assumed that I was out of its path. Never apply logic to ghosts.

I switched on the kitchen light and spied some clean glasses still drying on the wooden dish drainer. I filled one with water. As I drank, I leaned against the front rim of the sink and gazed out of the large window above it. Outside, the unlit backyard was a shadowy hodgepodge of craggy palms and inky Spanish moss. Beside my grandmother's crumbling stone patio, our 200-year-old oak loomed like a spectral giant waiting to eat Jack and his beanstalk. That tree had been my childhood friend.

A rumble shattered my daydream: the vertical blinds in front of me began to rattle and sway as if attacked by a small hurricane. Was the ceiling fan on? I glanced up. The fan blades were still, while a few feet away, the window blinds flapped and spun wildly. My eyes raced over everything around the window, searching frantically, but seeing nothing. The air felt heavy and poisonous.

As I whirled around to face the open doorway, an icy gale smashed straight into my face. On its back rode a murderous demonic entity. Raging beyond reason, it raced straight at me through the alcove. I was cornered. Or was I?

> *Be sober; be vigilant;*
> *because your adversary the devil,*
> *as a roaring lion, walketh about,*
> *seeking whom he may devour.*
> —1 Peter 5:8

The Bible verse popped into my head without warning. I didn't remember memorizing it; I hardly remember ever reading it before! Nonetheless, it was there and it gave me the kick I needed. *Be vigilant.* Why was I allowing myself to cower in a corner? I was sick and tired of being driven from room to room in my own house and constantly held captive in that cramped downstairs bedroom. *This is my home! It was my grandparents' home. Who pays the bills here, anyway? Not some bad-tempered demon, that's for sure.*

"Go away!" I growled out loud. I didn't want to wake Jack or Erin with ballistic shouting, but I wasn't going to leave my haunted kitchen without a fight. "YOU'RE

NOT WELCOME HERE! THIS IS NOT YOUR HOUSE! NOW, GET OUT OF MY WAY!"

With a huff, I turned my back on the demon, snapped off the kitchen light, and stomped out through the shadows of the breakfast nook, through the dark dining room, and into our bedroom. The villainous presence stayed in the kitchen. I could feel its eyes on my every step.

Clicking our bedroom's lock behind me, I peeked into Erin's crib, which stood in a corner between the door and our bed. My tiny sweetheart was lying safely on her back, snoozing away, cuddled in a dreamy quilt of sleep. Four feet away lay Jack with his back to me, apparently asleep as well. Everything seemed safe, so I pulled on my pajamas and tiptoed into the adjoining bathroom to brush my teeth. As my mouth foamed white with toothpaste, I glanced at the sparkling pink tile around the sink and bathtub. When I was a little girl, I used to think this room was made of cotton candy. What was the rest of this house made of, now?

I rinsed my mouth, walked out of the bathroom, and froze in terror. It couldn't be true. Not after all this time.

The demon was in our bedroom.

The air, which only seconds before had felt clear and fresh, was now liquid muck. Nothing looked out of the ordinary, but there was no doubt that the evil entity had somehow slithered in. I crept over to Erin's crib, placed my hand on her softly rising chest, and searched every inch of the room with my eyes. Something watched me. I glanced over my right shoulder at the door. In the center of its black wood, only four feet from my sleeping baby, floated a seething, disembodied, luminous face. Pure hate radiated around it like a blasphemous halo. I knew that face and it knew me. It was the same image I'd seen on the upstairs bedroom door on Christmas Eve when I was eight years old. There were the same vicious eyes, the same pointed nose diving into the same pointed chin; the same cavernous, rubber mouth dripping up and down and side to side in an eternal hysterical silent scream. I was looking into the face of a demon—a demon that was a breath away from my sleeping baby.

I slammed my fist against the cursed door and began waving it all over the surface in a panic-stricken effort to wipe out the Face. It leered out at me, unscathed. I could feel the evil pressing against my hand as I glanced into my daughter's crib. Erin never stirred from her deep sleep. I counted her every breath.

A luminous, swirling mist then filled our bedroom. On the far side of the room by my husband—who still appeared to be asleep—billowed an ashen, cloudy pillar about five feet high. I somehow knew it was female. I desperately hoped it was an angel. Her maternal sympathy, albeit detached, empathized with my agony. Neither of us had any idea how to protect my child from the demon. Although the female spirit was unable to move or aid me in any way, she offered me the only thing she could: hope. *Keep fighting, Vivian. Nothing can beat a mother tiger.*

I gazed in amazement at the swarming nightmare. *This place is a circus*, I hysterically thought to myself, *with that demonic, sneering face as ringmaster!* I planted my hand against the possessed door, determined to remain by Erin's crib until I had found a way to stop this super-natural nonsense. I was far from giving up.

God is more powerful than anything!

My mother's wise words flashed in my mind. Yes, *anything*. That was my salvation: trust God. Trust Him like I'd never trusted anything before in my life. With my right arm still protectively covering my sleeping baby, I bowed my head over her crib and began to fervently and frantically pray.

In a few minutes, our bedroom was clear. The drip-ping face and snarling fog had disappeared and was re-placed by an overwhelming sense of absolute peace. God's protection blanketed everything. Most importantly, Erin was safe, guarded by a power greater than my weak human hands could ever offer. I lifted my hand from her, bent to kiss her soft little cheek, then crawled back into bed beside Jack and fell into a deep, quiet, and confident sleep. I had considered "the peace that passes understand-ing" as only a cute Sunday School rhyme, but that night I learned that the power was real and far stronger than any earthly terror. God had delivered us; all I had to do was trust and pray. Really, truly pray. No nursery rhymes, no waving crucifixes, no lighting candles. Just honest, gut-wrenching prayer. That was the ticket.

Initially, I said nothing to Jack about the late-night chaos, but after a couple of clear, peaceful days and nights, I began to feel hopeful that our demon was really gone for good. Still, I didn't dare let Erin out of my sight for one moment. My late nights alone in the front room were over. If I was still wakeful after Erin fell asleep at night, I turned on the TV set in our bedroom and put it on mute. There was seldom anything worth hearing on TV anyway. But I missed reading my books under the living room light.

"By the way," I casually ventured to Jack during dinner one evening, "did you know that our ghosts returned with a vengeance the other night? I was falling asleep in our bed when I glanced toward our bedroom door and I saw…"

"…a man with a pointed chin floating on our bedroom door," Jack interrupted, never looking up from his plate.

I was stunned and frightened. I had never told my husband about my childhood encounter with the Face on Christmas Eve. "You saw him, too? I thought you were asleep the whole time. You never moved."

"I was asleep," Jack quickly answered, "but I woke up when you came in the bedroom."

"If you saw that face by Erin's crib, then why didn't you get up?"

"I wasn't sure at the time if I was dreaming or not." Jack reasoned. "After you got up and stood by Erin's crib, it seemed to fade away, so I just shut my eyes and went back to sleep."

"But, Jack, how could you ..."

"I have to finish installing that new sink in the up-stairs bathroom!" Jack retreated up the stairs and in a few minutes the house rocked with angry hammering. My husband might not admit it, but he was as scared as I was.

Jack's fingers frantically flew across the keyboard as a green gaggle of alien aircraft and starships zoomed drunkenly across his computer screen. ZAP! BOOM! Space Captain Jack had saved the day again!

Compared to the weird things that romped around our house, the world of computer games was a welcome reality to Jack. My earlier rebuke had been followed by a haunted hour of that misty woman glaring at him from the hall. It seemed Jack was plagued by reprimanding women from all dimensions.

WHUMP—WHAM! Jack jumped out of his seat. What the heck was that? His computer never made noises like that. He wasn't even touching the keyboard now.

RRRRRRR—BOOM!

Jack peered out into the dark hallway. The stairway was empty. Even the glaring woman was gone. From the far end of the upstairs corridor, the bathroom convulsed, then spat out a noise that rolled out the door and up the hall to the foot of Jack's study door.

"I don't believe it." Jack muttered to himself. "The ghosts are bowling."

Jack clicked on the hall light and walked into the bathroom. He had started the lavatory's overdue renovation that morning by pulling out the industrial pedestal sink and dumping it out the back door. Only an empty hole in the white tile floor remained where the unsightly basin had stood. Although I guarded most of my old house's authentic pieces as if they were my own children, we agreed long ago that the bathroom washbowl, along with the dismal Spanish Inquisition light fixtures, were some of the few original fixtures that had to go. They were just too ugly for anyone to endure for another seventy years.

Satisfied that the silent bathroom would stay that way, Jack returned to his study and sat again at his desk. WHAP! Another invisible bowling ball crashed against the bathroom's tile wall and audibly rolled down the hallway toward Jack's open office door. He stared in amazement. All of the upstairs lights were on, and there were no bowling balls in sight. Yet the lavatory and hall crashed and boomed. What the heck were those ghosts tossing around in the bathroom—and out at Jack?

Jack marched down the hall for a second look. All was calm; all was bright. The hole in the bathroom floor was still there. His back still ached from hauling that deadweight fixture all the way down the stairs and out the back door … that was it! The ghosts were mad because that ugly sink was gone! Those clunks weren't the sound of bowling balls; it was the spectral sink continually being rolled out of the bathroom, down the hall, and tossed all over the place in angry protest. Jack was being cursed for his home improvement work.

Shaking his head in dismay, Jack returned to the study, sank into his chair, and resumed his computer game. The first hostile spaceship flashed across the screen. Jack leaned forward, thumb poised on the joystick: ready, aim … WHUMP! The rattling floorboards shook Jack's flip-flop sandals off of his feet as another invisible sink crashed down the hall and merrily bounced down the stairs, one step at a time. BUMP! BUMP! WHAP! With a resolved sigh, Jack returned to the bathroom. Silence. Jack walked back to the study. BOOM! CRASH! Jack ran back down the hall; the bathroom was as clean and tidy as a new bottle of Clorox bleach. Jack returned to the study.

The ghostly bowling Olympics continued longer than the clock had hours to strike. While Jack spent the entire night frantically chasing bouncing phantom bathroom fixtures, Erin and I snored soundly downstairs in the bedroom. We never heard a squeak.

The next morning's sun was still yawning when Jack shot out of our front door. He had never been so happy to leave on an overnight business trip in his life. In his hurry, he accidently-on-purpose forgot to tell me about the previous night's spectral bowling party. Ignorant of our ghosts' demeanor, Erin and I snuggled down for a girls' slumber party. By some miracle, Erin decided to fall asleep by eight that night, and I was left in the delightful position of having quality time to myself. Our shared downstairs bedroom had been silent and clear since the demon face had disappeared two nights before; so, with a brand-new night light shining next to Erin's crib, I confidently closed the door to our bedroom and snuggled with my faithful big book into Grandma Jenny's century-old loveseat in the next room. Only one wall separated my sleeping child and me; her crib was literally on the opposite side of my sofa. She was so close that I could hear her snoring through the closed door. Surely I could keep an eye on her from this distance. The house was peaceful. Disturbingly peaceful.

Maternal intuition jarred me from my reading. Something wasn't right in the adjoining bedroom. I could feel it. Tossing my book on the floor, I leapt from my seat and cracked open the door to peek in on my baby. Cold, inky blackness slapped my face. Who had turned off the night light? I swung the door open, allowing the light from the living room to spill in. My eyes swooped down to my baby, still sleeping peacefully in her crib beside the door. I gently touched her warm, soft arm and pulled her little blanket over her bare feet. Erin and her bed felt safe, as if a bubble of love and warmth protectively surrounded her. Nothing could harm or even touch her. My prayers were still being answered. I bent over my baby to give her one more kiss.

A freezing chill spilled onto the top of my head, slithered down the back of my shirt, and burrowed into the base of my spine. I looked up. Three feet directly over my baby hung the gigantic spider shadow that tried to bar my husband from the kitchen the previous spring. I leaned down over Erin, using my body to shield her. The shadow dropped another six inches toward my child, poised to spring on its tiny prey. It seemed to know that it couldn't penetrate the protective bubble, but it was patient. Something would eventually change, allowing it to pounce.

Rage obliterated my fear. Just as I had acted with the demonic face two nights before, I waved my arms straight through the mucky spidery mass and started praying, praying, praying. The mammoth spider abruptly sprung straight up to the ceiling and clung upside down, still hovering over the crib. Ha! So it was a coward after all! My raging mother-tiger mode kicked into full gear: I climbed onto the side of the crib rail and stretched my arms up as high as they would go without snapping out of their sockets. My hands smashed through the foggy black body, grasping and clawing wildly at the frigid mass; I felt dusty plaster fill the tips of my fingernails as they scraped against the cracked ceiling.

"Please, dear God, make it go away!"

All at once, the spider shadow vanished. Dizzy with adrenaline, I stepped down from the teetering crib's side and bent over my child once again. Still soundly asleep, a dreamy smile drifted across her pink lips as I softly kissed her.

"Don't worry about anything," I whispered to my slumbering baby. "Mommy is right here by your side with your guardian angel. God is watching over all of us. Nothing will ever hurt you in this house. God and I won't let it. I promise."

May 21, 1995

"JAAA-AAACK!"

The sonorous tone sang out mockingly from the ceiling corner above Jack's head. He heard the deep voice very clearly. It began on a lower note then rose like a murderous school bully mocking a helpless young child.

"JAAA-AAACK!"

Trembling, Jack slowly raised his eyes upward toward the sound of the voice. Deserted cobwebs swayed silently from the corner where something sneered down at him. Jack had been innocently groping through one of our many over-stuffed bookcases, searching for his beloved volume of *Sherlock Holmes*. He hadn't bet on Moriarty greeting him.

"JAAAA…"

Jack bolted straight out of the dining room, through our front door, and dashed down the blood-red brick street toward the lake where Erin and I sat feeding the ducks. He didn't say one word to me about the disembodied voice. To be honest, I didn't tell him about the orange perfumed female phantom that had been sitting with Erin and I and the ducks. The difference was that the ghostly lady at the lake was *nice*.

I was worried. Something evil was infiltrating our house. We had to get rid of it, but bringing an Ouija board into the house or contacting a paid psychic from the nearby spiritualist town, Cassadega, was out of the question. We trusted neither and suspected both choices would only aggravate our already weird situation.

I wailed to Jack's mom over the phone, "What am I going to do? I can't let those stupid spooks get my baby, but I won't abandon my family home, either. What's wrong with me?"

"There's not a thing wrong with you!" Margaret Miller firmly consoled me. "And don't you *dare* let them run you out of your own house. Fight back! Get those white candles like I told you and place them in every single room. Get an extra large one and place it next to Erin's crib. Those lit candles will call protective angels to guard her from that demon. In the meantime, I'm going to make a copy of a special protective prayer for children and send it to you. Hang that on the wall at the head of my granddaughter's crib. With God's help, we're going to beat these demons!"

Night was falling once again, and I was frantic. I tore into the nearest grocery store and grabbed every white candle on the shelf. An hour later, our candle-stuffed house was glowing like a bonfire. I placed ten in our bedroom alone, with the fattest, biggest alabaster candle stuck right next to Erin's crib. I expected to hear the Orlando Fire Department chopping down our front door any minute.

Jack was on another overnight business trip, so Erin and I were alone with our candles and whatever else walked through our house. (I still had no idea that a disembodied voice had sent Jack running out the front door so fast the previous day that he forgot to close it behind him.) I tucked my baby into her crib. Our bedroom glowed in silver white candlelight. I switched off the light, confident of lasting peace and protection.

But the darkness had other ideas. A paranormal cacophony flocked straight to the candles like fire-immune moths! My promised protective angels were lost in the misty hurricane that danced around a smoky cloud pillar. Hatred and murder radiated throughout the room. Every entity in our house silently bellowed, "How dare you attempt to drive us out! Do you really think that these little white wicks of wax would get rid of us?" It was true; the flickering candles poured gasoline on the spectral fire. Worst of all, the dripping demon face was back.

"Something wicked this way comes…" I blurted out to myself. "No, forget that. It's here already! Oh, God, what am I going to do?"

You... are from God and have overcome them,
because the One who is in you is greater than
the one who is in the World.

Huh? Where had *that* come from? I could almost hear that remote verse that my mother had quoted to me since childhood. It was I John 4:4. I took the hint and grabbed the Bible my parents had given to me. With a prayer for guidance, I flipped it open and read aloud the first verse that I saw:

For we wrestle not against flesh and blood, but
against principalities, against powers, against
the rulers of the darkness of this world, against
spiritual wickedness in high places.
—Ephesians 6:12

Yeah, that sounded like what was in my bedroom, alright! I grabbed another chunk of pages and read the first words I saw:

... This kind can only come out by the power
of prayer.
—Mark 9:29

My eyes skipped up a few lines:

Everything is possible for him who believes.
—Mark 9:23

God had knocked me in the head. How could I have been so stupid? How could I have ever thought that I alone could battle evil spirits? Between the candles and nursery rhymes, I had left out the only true thing that worked—prayer. What was the one thing that had made that spider shadow curl up into a ball? Prayer. What had gotten the face on our door to go away that one night? Prayer. I had to turn this whole paranormal mess over to God. I bowed my head over sleeping Erin's crib.

After a few prayerful minutes, I opened one eye and peeked around the room. I couldn't believe it! The spooky, swirling mist and cloudy pillar had disappeared. The room felt clear of every evil spirit. I never felt so humbled or grateful in my life.

Thank God.

six

More Unexpected Guests

Orlando, Florida:
1996–present

Little Girl Lost

"Who's your new friend, Erin?"

Jack didn't recognize the somber little girl standing a few feet from where five-year-old Erin was playing with some of her toys on the floor of our front room. Usually Erin played in her own bedroom or in the down-stairs playroom, but today she was trying to find a quiet spot away from her one-year-old baby sister's perpetually grabbing little hands. Jack was happy to see that his older daughter had a new playmate, although he didn't remember the doorbell ringing or anyone mentioning that she were expecting a friend to come over.

The little girl looked about six or seven years old, just a bit older than Erin, with long brown hair and pretty ringlets around her face. The late September sunlight shone through the open window, bathing both girls in a warm amber glow. The kids had been playing dress-up: the new girl was wearing an old-fashioned pinafore apron over her silver-gray dress. Jack wondered why usually generous Erin wasn't sharing her dolls with her new friend. Erin was usually eager to include everyone in her games and it was obvious from the little girl's expression that she desperately wanted to join in the fun. Perhaps she was shy and was waiting for a verbal invitation.

"Who's your new friend, Erin?"

No sooner had the words left Jack's mouth than the little girl abruptly crumpled up like a newspaper and vanished into thin air.

"Did you say something, Daddy?" Erin never looked up from her pile of dolls.

"Uh…never mind." Trembling, Jack left the room. There was no point in saying anything to his young daughter about what he'd just seen. Why scare her? She'd been so engrossed in her play that she was oblivious to everything going on around her, including his repeated questions about the "new friend." Erin was in no danger.

As long as she wasn't aware of her ghostly new pal, what was the harm in letting the lonely little spirit watch?

The "little girl ghost" was to become our permanent visitor. Jack spotted her in the downstairs playroom, staring longingly at our children's dress-up box overflowing with floppy garden-party hats and pink plastic shoes and costumes created from every child's daydream. Once, as I rushed past the upstairs hallway balancing an armload of clean laundry, I caught a glimpse of her playing in Erin's bedroom. She was sitting quietly on the floor, surrounded by little ceramic teacups and a blue fluffy Easter bunny. Her veil of sad loneliness hovered about her, despite the toys. Three blinks later, she was gone. The sunlit room felt as forlorn as the toy teacup she left behind.

The following spring, Jack spotted her standing alone under my parents' magnolia tree in the front yard. Jack had just taken Baby Elise and Erin inside of our house to dry off after an afternoon swim in their inflatable yard pool. The little girl was staring longingly at the tempting water in front of her. Three small brown leaves floated down and landed in the pool's center, spinning mockingly in the cool water. Dead leaves could play there, but not her.

Our family became fond of this little phantom, although she still gave us the willies from time to time. Jack jumped out of his skin one evening when he turned on the breakfast nook light to discover the little girl sitting at our table, staring straight at him with wide, luminous eyes. Another late evening, the spectral girl surprised Jack on the couch while he was watching TV. Trying to follow my perpetual advice that he should try to make friends with the little spirit rather than run from her, Jack kept his cool and mustered a smile. A tiny red ball, very solid and very real, suddenly rolled across the floor and bumped to a stop at Jack's feet. We didn't own a red ball. The spectral child giggled. That was more than poor Jack's nerves could handle for that night. He promptly bolted upstairs to bed, and the red ball was never seen again.

On nights when Erin had trouble falling asleep, I would settle myself in Great-Grandma Jenny's rocker armed with a fat book. During these quiet, peaceful evenings, the little girl ghost would peek over my shoulder with a playful "I'm here!" look. She must have wanted me to read her a bedtime story from my book, but I doubted that she would find Maya Angelou or Ernest Hemingway as entertaining as Cinderella. I wished I could wrap my arms reassuringly around her transparent little body and hug away the sadness in her sweet smile.

One late May evening, I woke up at two in the morning on the dot wondering why Erin was playing in the hall outside of our bedroom door. If my daughter woke up in the middle of the night, she headed straight to our bed for comfort; if she chose to play, it was always quietly in her own room, where she wouldn't be heard and told to go back to sleep. Although the words were muffled, I could clearly hear a little girl's voice happily chattering away to herself like children do when they're absorbed in a pretend world. I rolled out of bed, staggered across our large bedroom, and opened the door to steer my child back to her bed. The house was suddenly as quiet as cotton and, of course, the brightly lit hallway was completely empty. I peeked into Erin's room: she was sound asleep with her trusty night light beside her.

After that night, the little spirit crept into our bedroom at night and stood beside me as I slept, patiently waiting for me to wake up and notice her. I would open my eyes with a start, expecting to see my daughter's face. I wouldn't *see* the little girl in these cases, but I never needed to. I knew when she was around. One night, I awoke to her voice calling out to me from the hallway: "Momm-meeee! Mommm-meeee!" When I reached the hall, her voice had drifted into Erin's bedroom. I opened the door and found my sleeping child in the middle of a pitch black room. Her night light had been turned off. My daughter hated the dark; had Erin woken up, she would have been hysterical with fear. Were it not for the little girl's voice calling to me, I wouldn't have discovered the problem. As I switched the bedside lamp on, I wondered who had turned it off. Did the little girl do it as a prank to get my attention, or did something darker deliberately extinguish it? Had the child spirit woke me up to protect her friend?

A few days later, as I dressed Erin for school, she and I heard a child's soft voice calling through the house:

"Mommy! Mommy!" We knew who it was. She wasn't calling for her own mother, but simply addressing me by the only name that she knew me by. I was "mommy" in our house.

The little ghost has called out to me—and only to me—ever since. Her voice is never distressed; she simply wants my attention, just like my other children. She ran up excitedly behind me in the kitchen while I was stirring Christmas cookie batter and two months later she mischievously swiped some chicken nuggets that were cooling for Elise's lunch. Bottles of eye drops disappeared from my bedside table, only to reappear a week later exactly in the same spot. On three separate occasions, Jack, myself, and fifteen-year-old Ian watched a decorative wicker basket levitate a foot straight out from the top of the refrigerator and hang for a split second in thin air before dropping to the floor. Crashes would erupt from the children's empty playroom; I would rush in to find everything in order except for a stack of books piled neatly in the middle of the room, beside the empty bookshelf where they had just been resting. Piles of paper would float horizontally off my desk, hang for a moment in midair, then float gently all over the room before my eyes. The ceiling fan blades in my bedroom would turn around and around and around, even though the wires had been clipped years ago.

And our little girl ghost liked doors. She liked to knock on doors. She liked to open doors. Her hobby began with

Erin's bedroom door one evening while Jack was reading our older daughter her nightly bedroom story:

"I do not like green eggs and ham; I do not like them, Sam I—"

Knock knock.

"Come on in. We're just reading Dr. Seuss."

Knock knock.

Jack leaned over from his seat and pulled open Erin's closed door. The hall was empty. Jack shut the door and resumed his reading:

"I would not, could not, with a goat—"

Knock knock.

Little Erin grinned as she watched her exasperated father once again answer her door in vain. She knew who was knocking, but she wasn't going to tell Daddy. That would ruin the game. The knocking continued nightly, always and only when Jack was reading to Erin in her room. Ian and I chuckled with Erin at their gullible father, who always seemed to be the brunt of the latest paranormal prank. After a week, Jack's humor was gone. He fumed at the empty hall. An angry father meant that bedtime was no fun for Erin anymore, so I came up with a plan.

The next afternoon, Ian and I stood outside Erin's room and I announced in a loud voice, "OK, Ian, whenever you hear a knock on your door, don't answer or even open it. If it's Dad or me, we'll just walk right in after we knock—but be sure to let out a yell first if you're not dressed!" Apparently, the little girl ghost was listening, because bedtime was never again interrupted by knocking on the doors. She just switched door tricks ...

Knock knock knock.

Jeff the plumber stood on our front porch, waiting for someone to open the big wooden door. He'd already rung the doorbell twice, but every time he pushed the button, it was as silent as an obstinate child. Jeff decided that it must be broken—like everything else in this big old house. Two days ago, our family had arrived home from a weekend trip to find that a fickle pipe under our downstairs bedroom had burst. Our front yard was now a small lake. Jack had waded through our soppy grass and phoned Jeff about our plumbing problem. He forgot to mention our ghost problem.

Inside and upstairs, I was vaguely aware of a faraway tapping. The dense lathe and plaster walls swallowed any outside noise quieter than a sledgehammer. I had been keeping an ear out for the plumber that morning, but he had run late and I was now distracted by a huge pile of laundry.

Pound! Pound! BAM!

Outside Jeff was getting impatient with good reason. Someone was obviously at home. Our van was parked in the driveway and Jeff could hear footsteps wandering around on the other side of the closed door.

"Be right there!" I called out from my upstairs bedroom. The knocking noise had finally reached our second floor. As I descended the staircase, Jeff spied me through the small upper window on the front door and waved with relief. There was no need for me to rush; I'd skidded down these slippery steps flat on my tailbone one too many times in my life. Anyone who dared to go faster than a crippled snail risked becoming a runaway bobsled, possibly at the invisible hands of our bullying female ghost. As I raised my hand to return Jeff's wave, a loud CLICK reverberated through the house. From my spot at the top of the stairs, I had a straight, clear view of the front door. To my horror and embarrassment, the deadbolt snapped open and the doorknob began to turn by itself.

"No! Wait! Stop!" I whisper-screamed at the slowly opening door. Jeff gave me a quizzical look through the door's window. Panic stricken, I swung myself around the top banister, skidded over the sharp stairway landing, and jumped down the remaining steps to the ground floor in two painful leaps. My efforts were in vain. The door had already creaked open wide enough to expose the face of our very confused plumber staring wide-eyed from the porch. I slid across the living room floor and slammed straight into the massive wayward door.

WHAM!

With a way-too-wide smile plastered on my bruised face, I grabbed the door's corner and pretended to open it the rest of the way myself.

"Hi, Jeff!" I squealed. "I guess you found our hidden key under the doormat and let yourself in, great, right, let me show you where this leak is …"

Jeff's jaw was on the floor. "I—I never touched the door. It just opened by itself! I swear, I stood here watching you walk down the stairs, then the latch opened and the door swung open and nobody was there."

I shrugged. "Yeah, well, this door does that sometimes, but let me show you where this leak is …" As I dragged our baffled plumber through the doorway and into our haunted house, a very cold little spot followed at my heels. I'd have to talk with the girl about not opening the door to strangers.

Two weeks later, mountains of teetering grocery bags stuffed to the brim threatened to break my forearms as I staggered along my red brick front walk. Balancing large overflowing brown bags is a circus act attempted by every hungry person who has ever grocery shopped. Groaning under the bags' bulk, I gingerly placed one foot on the first of our three front porch steps, praying for balance. My view of the ground was obliterated by food.

"Sure would be nice if someone would open the front door for me," I groaned. My plea was more of an empty complaint than a request, since no one was inside my dark, locked house. No sooner had I spoken than the front door knob merrily turned and our massive door swung wide open for me.

"Thank you!" My gratefulness was understated, since my house key was at the bottom of my purse, which was at the bottom of the splitting grocery bag. I stepped into our front room, expecting to see Erin's little head bob out from behind the door. The grinning girl I spotted was not my daughter. With a shy smile and a nod of her long, brown corkscrew curls, she vanished.

"Thank you!" I quickly called after her. Her delighted smile permeated the air. She had helped "mommy."

My gratitude made a big impression. For the next several weeks, the little girl obligingly opened the front door for me whenever I came home loaded with groceries. I didn't always see her, but there was no doubt who my little invisible helper was. We delighted in playing our sweet and slightly spooky little game; I actually found myself making excuses to go to the market. I had such fun that I was absolutely stunned when Jack walked in the house one day, visibly shaking with nerves.

"The front door just opened by itself! It was *bolted* and I pointed my key toward the lock, when the door knob turned from the inside and..."

I glanced at the small Walgreen's drug store bag he held in his quivering left hand.

"You just came from the store, right? For weeks, the little girl has been opening the door for me when I'm dragging in groceries. Why are you upset? Did you at least thank her for helping you?"

Jack groaned. "I was too surprised to speak!"

"Well, thank her!" I ordered.

Jack looked as if I'd lost my mind. "Excuse me, but I'm not used to invisible doormen, as you apparently are. Next time, keep me up to date on what the latest ghostly game is. Honestly, Viv, you're acting as if you were defending one of our own kids. Remember, however endearing she may be, this kid is a *ghost.*" Jack sighed. "OK ... I promise to try to remember to show my gratitude next time."

But there was no next time. After Jack's loud complaint, the front door never opened for any of us again, no matter how desperately I pleaded from behind grocery bags.

My dad bent over his wooden workbench, intent on finishing his latest battleship model. Seventy-five years ago, he had been born Philip J. MacPherson, but his granddaughter Erin had dubbed him Poppy when she was two years old. The name stuck and was added to his other array of family nicknames: Jack called him Captain Dad, and I just kissed and hugged him as Daddy. His real title should have been Sir Skeptic.

Daddy's favorite hobby was hand-carving models of Navy LCI World War II ships. A proud veteran of the Invasion of Normandy (his ship landed at Gold Beach on that historic day), my dad had spent his retirement years hand-carving intricate models of these famous vessels, many of which are displayed in Naval museums across our country. Since my parents' current apartment was too small to accommodate his piles of saws and tools, his workshop (nicknamed the Shipyard) was stationed on our house's side screened porch. It had become his second home, and we loved having him around.

Daddy's only blueprints were the original 1940s war photos of each individual ship that his customers mailed to him with their order. Each detailed model took weeks, often months, to complete, and my dedicated artist father regularly spent fifteen-hour days happily immersed in his work, stopping only to grab another bag of popcorn from our nearby kitchen. I was so proud of my talented dad!

During his long days in his workshop, Daddy kept his cell phone close beside him, placed carefully in an exact spot. One night, as he was preparing to leave, Daddy waved me over to his workbench. His face was perplexed.

"I can't seem to find my cell phone. I was just talking with a customer on it a few minutes ago, and I could swear that I put it back right here on the table. I probably knocked it on the ground. Could you help me take a look around?" For the next hour, we searched every inch of the side porch as well as several interior rooms in our house. Defeated, I slowly walked my dad to our front door.

"I'm sorry, Daddy," I sighed, "but your phone just isn't anywhere around here."

No sooner had I spoken than a ringing sound drifted in from the side porch. On the workbench lay the elusive cell phone in its proper spot, merrily ringing away. A moment ago, that table had been empty. As my father reached to answer it, the ringing stopped. There was no log of the call recorded in the phone's memory.

"It's the ghost!" I laughed. "She's playing a trick on you because you won't believe that she really is around here!" My father chuckled good-naturedly; he was too delighted to have his precious phone back to argue with my claim—but he still didn't believe a word of it.

A few weeks later, Daddy's phone disappeared *again*. This time we searched not only the side porch, but also every inch of our own home, my parents' apartment, and even my dad's car. The search continued, off and on, for over four months until Daddy finally admitted defeat and bought a new cell phone. The following evening, he opened the front door of his car, climbed into the driver's seat, started the engine, glanced to his right, and discovered, laying quietly in the middle of the front passenger seat, his prodigal phone! He immediately dialed my number.

"I don't want to hear one word about ghosts!" my dad growled good-naturedly at me. "That was a good trick you guys played on me. I just wish you hadn't let it go on so long."

I sighed. "Daddy, you looked through this house with us. For heaven's sake, why would any of us hide your phone? I tell you, it's the ghost! She's just picking on you because you won't admit that she's real!"

Daddy laughed. "Well, whatever happened, I sure won't leave any more of my things in that kooky house of yours!"

A year later, the darn phone was again in peril. My dad accidentally dropped it in the middle of Erin's elementary school carnival but didn't notice it was gone until we had climbed into his car to drive back home. Our family search party turned over every pebble on the school's grounds, but this time it looked as if the phone really was gone for good. Daddy switched to his second, back-up cell phone, but he still missed his favorite first phone. The fat lady still hadn't sung her last note in my book; I decided to dial the missing cell's phone number to see if it was still working and, more importantly, to find out who or what might answer. After several rings, the sound of my father's disembodied voice on his recorded phone mail greeting eerily came on. Uncertain of what else to do, I left a message:

"Uh, hi! This is Vivian Campbell. If anyone finds this phone and hears this message, please call me back. This is my dad's phone and he really needs it. Thanks!"

The following afternoon, Daddy called me from his car. I was surprised to hear from him, since he had just driven away from our house after spending a long afternoon at his beloved work bench.

"You have a *weird* house!" he exclaimed. "Guess what I'm talking on right now?"

I didn't need a second guess. "Your favorite cell phone."

"Vivian, I looked over at the passenger seat just now and there it was!"

My matter-of-fact, PhD father was never at a loss for a logical explanation, but this time he was stumped.

"Daddy, this is the third time our little girl ghost has found and returned your phone. Now, what do you have to say to that?"

"That you have a *weird* house!"

Who is this nameless little sprite? Is she a past resident of the house? My best guess is no. My spirit-sensitive friends and I all agree that she is a child from the past—probably the 1930s—who lived in our neighborhood, but not in our house. Maybe she played here as a child, or perhaps she—like our many of the other resident wandering souls—is just drawn to our house as a place of security. My ghost-sensitive friend Kristina has often commented that our house is "very spiritual." In other words, we live in Ghost Mecca. Lucky us!

Mrs. Wickham

In the midst of my chatting guests, Mrs. Wickham glared from her place on my grandmother's Victorian loveseat where she sat primly with her hands folded tightly in her lap. She had not been invited to my tea party. But she was dead. She came anyway.

"Mrs. Wickham is *not* amused!" my friend Nell snickered at me through the kitchen door.

"So what else is new?" I plopped another dollop of mayonnaise in the middle of the egg salad I was frantically mixing for my tea sandwiches. Reaching for the jar of pickle relish, I smiled, secretly pleased that my house's ghostly matriarch had crashed another one of my parties. She'd been bumping around with us from the beginning and beyond. We could always count on Mrs. Wickham's constant disapproval of the way we took care of "her" house and encroached on her personal space.

It began one evening as I was changing our younger daughter's diaper in our upstairs bedroom. Jack burst into the room and thrust his bare arm in front of my face. "I have goosebumps!" he proclaimed like a Code Blue alert.

"Which ghost is it this time?" I yawned as I plunged my hand into a bin of diaper wipes.

"That old lady was standing in front of the fireplace waving at me!" Jack wailed.

I exploded in laughter. "She was *what?*"

Jack was not amused.

"It was Mrs. Wickham or whatever you call her. The same one that I saw standing on the front porch and later staring at me through the dining room window. I haven't seen her in over a year, but just now I walked into the front room and there she was, standing by the fireplace, waving at me!"

I handed Jack a drippy diaper and hiked downstairs to the front room. Sure enough, the room was noticeably colder, despite my feet frying from the heated floor vents. I walked over to the freezing fireplace and sat down on the piano bench. Mrs. Wickham stood nearby. She wasn't waving at me. She never greeted her competition.

I cleared my throat and folded my hands in my lap. "Mrs. Wickham, I know we don't see eye to eye on a lot of things—not that I can *see* your eyes, to begin with— but we're both moms and you're a grandmother as well, so we do agree on children. I've seen you bending over Elise's crib while she sleeps. Now, I understand that you were just checking on her, but if she had woken up and seen you, she would have been terrified, and I know you don't want that. So you're welcome to wander around the first floor to your heart's content, but after the girls are in bed, please don't go upstairs. Is that a deal, from one mom to another?"

The ghost considered my proposal and then vanished. From that night on, Mrs. Wickham kept her end of the bargain and stayed downstairs, but she had no patience for any of our family members who intruded on her ground floor after bedtime. Jack was the chief offender; my night owl husband rarely left his comfy TV chair before midnight. When he did bother to wander upstairs to bed, Mrs. Wickham followed at his heels to the top step. If he returned downstairs to the kitchen for a glass of water or a late night book, she wouldn't relax until he was snoring upstairs.

My late-night transgressions, while not as frequent as Jack's, were far more serious in Mrs. Wickham's exasperated opinion. Every few months, I would pull out my great-grandmother's hand painted china, shine up her sterling silver, and throw a High Tea, to all my friends' delight and Mrs. Wickham's dismay. Our matronly phantom most definitely did not approve of the late hours I spent in "her" dining room fussing over the formal place settings and luncheon menus for the next day's party. She made every disagreeable effort to shoo me back to my bedroom, all to no avail. I ignored her.

Mrs. Wickham knew that something had to be done. Her solution came in the form of a small, red leather book.

It was no secret that the hero of my famous tea parties was the original 1928 edition of *How to Entertain at Home: 1000 Entertainment Ideas Compiled by the Editor of The Modern Priscilla*. This text had belonged to my maternal grandmother, Mary Hosie Campbell, and was passed down to me by my mother on the day I announced my first High Tea. Its brown, brittle pages held the secrets to the proper way to set a table for any occasion and to the true identity of an array of ancient cutlery and silverware. There was every recipe from children's birthday tea-cakes to royal wedding dinners. It was my Tea Party Bible and everyone knew I was lost without it, especially wicked Mrs. Wickham.

One very late tea party eve, it vanished. I had just laid it carefully between a stack of cut-glass fruit bowls and a package of napkins on my overloaded dining table, and then turned my back for a moment to search for a cake knife. When I returned, all I saw was an empty space on the lace tablecloth.

"Mrs. Wickham!"

The ghost replied with a smug smile of satisfaction.

"Oh, come on. Give it back!" I whined to the thief. "You know that I know you've got it."

Mrs. Wickham glared and crossed her arms over her ample bosom.

"Keep it, then!" I spouted angrily at her corner of the room. "'But I'm *not* going to bed until this table is set correctly. Your sticky fingers will only result in my staying down here all the longer."

The ghost and I stayed up until after three a.m. My book did not reappear.

Despite Mrs. Wickham's thievery, my next day's tea party was a success. Days after the last tea cup was washed and the table cloth folded away, I was still searching for my book.

"That stupid ghost won't give it back to me!" I loudly complained to my author pal Dave Lapham when he stopped by to pick up a photo of my house to use in his next book, *Ancient City Hauntings: More Ghosts of St.*

Augustine. "It's not her book. She's a *thief,* and I'm going to sit in this dining room every single night until she returns it."

Dave chuckled. He had heard so many tales about my resident spooks that he was on a first name basis with each of them. As he walked down my front walkway toward his car, Dave paused for a moment to glance back at my house. On a whim, he spoke out loud:

"Hey, Mrs. Wickham! You can follow me home if you want to. I don't have three kids and a cat and a lizard and seven guinea pigs like Viv, so you'll have some peace and quiet. Sue and I would be glad to have you. Well, at least I will. I guess I'd better check with Sue first. But, if you insist on staying here, I know that Viv would really appreciate you returning that book to her. It belonged to her grandmother and she's sentimental about it. Thanks!"

The next morning I glanced into my grandfather's barrister bookcase. The elusive red leather 1928 edition of *How to Entertain at Home* stood in its regular place as if it had never moved an inch. Good friends really are priceless, especially the ones who can sweet-talk a bad-tempered ghost!

Despite her late-night efforts at sabotage, Mrs. Wickham always enjoyed my tea parties and never missed one. These culinary gatherings were the stuff of legends, especially with Mrs. Wickham in attendance. The fact that her name wasn't on the guest list made no difference; as far as she was concerned, *she* was the rightful hostess of these events (which she could never quite recall having planned) and I was the maid. Our difference of opinion always resulted in tea time trauma.

"Mrs. Wickham's sitting smack in the middle of your guests in the living room," my friend Nell informed me as I worked in the kitchen, "and she doesn't have a clue as to what the heck's going on. I caught the glint of her form standing by the piano, but as I was about to take a photo of your mom and my grandma sitting together on the couch, Mrs. Wickham suddenly popped over beside me!"

"Well, I'm glad she made it," I smiled over the pots of steaming water. "For the first time she didn't show up at all last night to steal my grandmother's tea book or glare at me. I was getting a little worried about her. She's never missed a tea."

"I actually smelled her before I saw her," Nell continued. "I wasn't the only one, either. Several of your guests asked what marvelous new brand of air freshener you use, then became visibly perplexed as the fragrance moved on its own from place to place. It was too funny!"

"She's on the go, again," Jack exclaimed, peeking back into the front room. "Now she's sitting on the antique red-velvet loveseat, staring at Vivian's mom."

I didn't like that. "I'd better go out there and see what Mrs. Wickham's up to."

Leaving Nell to finish making the sandwiches, I walked into the next room and spotted Mrs. Wickham sitting on the loveseat, opposite and a little apart from my other guests, who had gathered themselves into a conversational semicircle. Her wavy outline in front of the sunlit window looked like luminous steam rising from a hot road, a sight that my other guests apparently didn't see or logically dismissed as a trick of the afternoon light. I smiled politely at the others across the room and quietly took a seat beside my invisible acquaintance. Nell was right: Mrs. Wickham was miffed. She had no idea what these other women were babbling about, much less who any of them were. Worst of all, they were all ignoring her! As their hostess, she should be the center of attention. She sat stiffly with her hands folded primly in her lap, her burning eyes glued on my unsuspecting mother.

"Your grandmother is very benevolent," my friend Kristina whispered as she passed by my seat on the haunted couch.

"My grandmother?" I asked, in surprise. I pointed to a photograph hanging on the wall behind us. "My grandmother's been dead for years and years. This is Mrs. Wickham. She built this house and thinks she still owns it."

The ghost stiffened her back.

"Whoever she is, she sure likes your tea parties!" Kristina laughed.

"Tea's on!" I announced. As I lead the group into the dining room, I picked up an extra cup and saucer on the sideboard and set it quietly between Nell's place and mine at the table. "Let's just see what happens," I winked at my friend as I filled Mrs. Wickham's cup.

"Where's her chair?" Nell whispered.

"Don't you think pouring tea for her is strange enough?" I muttered back.

My long-suffering guests either took no notice or were polite enough not to comment on my eccentric table habits. Everyone took their seats, with Nell and I flanking Mrs. Wickham's lonely cup. Tea was offered, sandwiches were served, and our cheerful conversation continued.

Five minutes later, Nell caught my eye and nodded toward Mrs. Wickham's full cup between us. "Bubbles!" she whispered. Sure enough, part of the cooled tea was covered in a layer of tiny, popping bubbles. Even weirder was the cup's position—it had been turned a quarter from where I had set it down only a moment before! Nell and I excused ourselves, rushed into the kitchen, and burst into giggles like two mischievous schoolgirls who had just caught their prude principal adjusting her girdle.

Mrs. Wickham was waiting for us when we returned to our seats. Her humor had not improved. Not only was she was insulted at not being offered a chair with her tea cup, she wanted me to abdicate my seat at the head of the table. *She* was the real hostess, after all. As usual, I ignored her scowl and focused my attention on my living guests, but Nell—who was not used to dealing with our eccentric phantom's temperament—dragged me into the kitchen for a second time.

"Mrs. Wickham needs to get a better attitude," Nell snapped as we stood in front of the refrigerator. "What's wrong with her? She's insulted and acts as if this is *her* party and *she's* the host and that you should step aside! She even blew bubbles in her tea, for heaven's sake! Talk about rude!"

I rolled my eyes in agreement. "She does this all the time," I replied with a sigh. "You should have seen what she did to me when I was trying to get ready for my last party. She's just a snoopy old bitty!"

Right on cue, the ghost popped in between us.

"Oh my gosh, now she's in here shoving into our conversation," Nell wailed.

I grinned impishly. "Let's shove her in the fridge."

Mrs. Wickham popped right back out of that conversation!

Later that evening, long after bedtime, I caught sight of the disgruntled ghost sulking on the sofa. "What's that old witch got to be upset about?" I muttered as I balanced another armload of tea-stained china from the dining table to the overflowing kitchen sink. Thanks to her, I had spent the afternoon juggling bubbling tea cups and confused guests. She was lucky I wasn't chanting exorcism rhymes at her.

I dumped my dishes, strolled over to her couch, and sat down next to her. "Look, I'm sorry if Nell and I offended you this afternoon. Honestly, we were glad to have you with us. To tell you the truth, I was a little worried that you were going to miss my party altogether since you didn't show up to harass me last night when I was setting the table. I stayed up an extra hour, just to annoy you! However, it was nice not to have to worry about my tea party book disappearing again."

Mrs. Wickham folded her hands in her lap. I continued our conversation. "Nell's right, you know. You really need to have a better attitude at my tea parties. I'm sorry that you can't be the hostess, but I'm always happy to have you as my guest. My parties aren't half as interesting without you."

"Who are you talking to?" Seventeen-year-old Ian stood in the doorway, on his way to take out the garbage.

"It's just Mrs. Wickham," I replied.

"She's here?"

"Nell and I upset her at the tea party this afternoon," I explained, "and I'm trying to apologize."

Ian rolled his eyes. "Why do you care what a *ghost* thinks?"

I laughed in surprise at myself. "Mrs. Wickham's been with us so long that I'm beginning to think of her as an eccentric invisible aunt rather than a ghost."

My sentiment seemed to appease Mrs. Wickham. As soon as I finished my sentence, she was gone. I was forgiven—or at least tolerated—until the next tea party.

Mrs. Wickham is my proof that not all ghosts are malevolent or scary or even placid. Some are downright charming … that is, once you get used to each other.

Mr. Creepy

"Would somebody *please* answer the door?"

"Why bother? There's nobody there!"

"I know that. Open it anyway. It makes them happy."

We had just returned from spending the Fourth of July weekend with Jack's family in upstate New York. Just like cockroaches that will undoubtedly invade your Florida house if you forget to spray before you leave for an extended time, a new ghost or two always seemed to assume squatter's rights during our absence.

"Just ignore it," Jack sighed as he flipped channels on the TV set in front of his feet. "That bell ringing happened to me last night. I ran to the door, but our front porch was as empty as it is right now."

"There it goes again! Didn't anybody else hear the doorbell that time?" I pleaded. "For heaven's sake, I was two rooms away and I heard it. Twice."

Elise looked confused. "But, Mom, that doorbell hasn't worked for as long as I can remember."

A week later, as I sat typing in our downstairs family room, I heard our drawbridge front door groan wide open, then slam shut with its usual sonic boom. "I guess Jack's home," I sighed to myself. My rare day of solitary bliss had apparently come to an abrupt end. Since early that morning, I had been absolutely, positively alone in my lovely old house. The girls were at a sleepover birthday party, and Jack swore that there was no way he could return from his business trip until the next morning. Apparently Jack had been wrong.

I was in the middle of a writing roll, so I hated to halt my creative train of thought to get up and greet my husband in the next room. I heard Jack's steady footsteps plod across the living room and then slowly ascend the stairs. From the sound of his feet, he must have been really tired from that trip. Sigh. *Poor Jack.*

Guilt got the best of me: I pushed myself away from the word processor and trotted into the front room. It was empty, but that was to be expected since I had heard Jack walk up the stairs...or, at least, most of the stairs. Had I heard footsteps go all the way up? I glanced at the top of the stairway. The door to Jack's home office was closed, silent and undisturbed. The upstairs hallway was dark. Hmm. I pulled back the curtain of a nearby window and peered out into our driveway. It was as empty as the rest of the house.

"Jack?" I called up the stairs. "Are you home?"

Silence.

"Hello?" I repeated.

Silence.

Good grief. After spending a lifetime in kooky houses, you'd think that by now I could tell the difference between a living visitor and a ghost. Annoyed, I returned to my typing.

Ten minutes later, the ceiling shook. Clunk. Clunk. Scraaaaape. Someone was moving furniture around in

Erin's second floor bedroom! I ran up the stairs and threw open her door. Silence. Shadows. Not a bed or a book was out of place. I closed the door and returned to my downstairs typing. Again.

As soon as my seat hit the desk chair—WHUMP! The house reverberated with the sounds of more heavy furniture scooting and scraping across my daughter's upper bedroom. Erin would have a fit if that stupid ghost damaged even one dust bunny in her private bedroom! I stomped to the foot of the stairs.

"Hey! Cut it out!"

Silence. For good measure, I climbed up one more time to check out Erin's room. Everything stood as innocently untouched as ever. I rubbed my aching head and walked downstairs for the third time in the last fifteen minutes. Stupid ghost.

That night, Mr. Creepy came calling.

I was still hard at work by myself, typing late into the night, when he popped in. One moment I was lost in my prose; the next, my personal space was obliterated by a six-foot shadow that loomed over my back like a school principal threatening to whack me over the head. A decade ago, I would have stuck my head under the rug, but now I knew that ghosts in our house were as common as dust.

"Back off!" I yelled, shoving my right elbow into the pit of his foggy, frigid stomach. "You're in the way of my screen!"

Shocked, the rude wraith vanished. A minute later, he was back again. His tenacity was almost as tedious as my own.

"I said *back off*!" Sizzling with anger, I took a 180-degree spin in my chair, jumped up, and shoved my face toward his sooty gray fog. "Don't you know about personal space?" I screamed. "Now, *get out!*"

The shadow retreated into the far corner of the room.

"I said out of the room," I spat between gritted teeth as I pointed toward the open door. "That corner is not *out*. *Out* means either you leave my premises entirely or I'm going to start praying!"

The ghost vanished. The next morning, he planted himself in the middle of the staircase to leer at me while I did the laundry. I regarded him as another dust bunny. Mr. Creepy, as I had appropriately dubbed him, was in despair. It seemed he couldn't understand why, just for once, I wouldn't agree to be a good sport and shriek in blind terror at the sight of him, madly tossing towels and sheets in my wake.

Our new cat, Savannah, never knew whether to walk around or through the ghost. She would sit one stair beneath Mr. Creepy, looking slightly fearful and quite irritated. Both ghost and cat were equally obstinate; neither would give way for the other. Savannah would only venture up the stairs after Mr. Creepy had decided to disappear for the day. I was her personal escort and most of the time ended up carrying Her Feline Majesty in my arms.

She never had a particular reason to go up the stairs; most of the time she would just stand triumphantly in the upstairs hallway for a few moments, savoring her victory, and then she would trot back downstairs to her food dish in the kitchen. Her game was simply to out-wait the ghost.

Savannah's stamina finally gave out one day when I was in a hurry and strode straight past her and through our rude wraith. Horrified, the poor cat ran off. Savannah never went up that staircase again until after Mr. Creepy got bored with sliding down the banister and disappeared to find another corner to haunt.

The man was dressed to perfection. Not a crease was out of place on his jet black tux. His dark, short hair was slicked back behind his protruding ears. He looked like a living version of a black-and-white photo straight out of the 1928 edition of *Gentlemen's Quarterly*. Wall Street would have swooned; King George would have bowed; sexy silent film star Louise Brooks would have fainted in anticipation. The only problem was that he was standing in the middle of our bathtub.

Erin's mouth dropped as she stood transfixed in horror with one hand clutching the etched glass doorknob. It was bad enough to find the unlocked bathroom occupied when she had to go—and she *really, really* had to go right now—but what do you do when a strange man in a tuxedo is standing in the middle of your shower? She doubted that the man would get very far with a bath, since he was fully clothed and facing away from the shower head. The water wasn't even turned on. He seemed fascinated, even mesmerized, by the gleaming wall of puke-green tile that surrounded him. Unaware that he was being watched by an eight-year-old girl, or even that he was standing in a bathtub, the man slowly turned his head toward the open doorway. He was lost. He was confused. He was dead.

"MOMMMMMMMMMMMEEEEEEEE!"

A blink later, Erin dragged me down the hall to show me...an empty bathtub. It was her first lesson in ghostly hide-and-go-seek. (Hint: the ghosts usually win.) The dapper bathtub man was apparently a pro at this game, since he hid himself so well that no one ever saw him again...at least, not until he came back with his pet wolf to visit Jack. Erin learned to play this game better than Jack and even better than the ghost.

The two voices mumbled incoherently through the stillness of our dark house. It was past two a.m., but I was wide awake, straining to understand the rise and fall of the spooky verbalizations. One was deep and dark. It was Mr. Creepy, the dapper bully who walked into our house on the Fourth of July and proceeded to irritate our cat and pop up in our bedrooms and stairways and bathtubs. I had hoped that he had worn himself out and was gone for good. I was wrong.

The other voice was distressingly easy to recognize: it was our little girl ghost.

Their tones rose and fell in heated conversation, but I couldn't make out one word. The muffled garble sounded as if they were behind an invisible, thick wall or speaking through big cushions jammed over their mouths. The disembodied pair floated only a few feet from where I lay in my bed. I could *almost* see their heads, but they weren't in my room. They were caught in some in-between—a Purgatory-type plane that happened to be in the same place, but apparently not the same dimension, as my bedroom. The adult man's continual murmur to the child froze my spine. He sounded like he was going to murder her if she didn't obey his command. I lifted my head from my pillow and cupped my hand over my ear to better catch the sound. The voices still made no sense, but I could interpret the inflection of their pitch the same way that I knew what Savannah wanted from me, even though I didn't speak one word of "cat."

Mummmmummerrrmuh—

The deep tone was deranged; the man was struggling to keep control.

Muhmuh! Mmmmuh—Oh! RRRRrrrrrrrrmmmmmmMMMMMmmmuh—

The child was terrified. She was pleading with him; trying to get him to change his mind about something, something about us, but he kept interrupting her, talking over her, threatening her if she didn't cooperate...

Whaaaauhhhhhmmmmm ... muhmuhmuhRRRR RRRRRRRRmuhmmmm—

I'd heard spirit voices before babbling unintelligibly like this. In our Atlanta apartment, I'd lain on my couch in the middle of a long night listening to a chorus of demonic voices chant and mutter and cackle. The next morning, I had burned my neighbor's pack of tarot cards that she'd left at my place. I never heard those same evil voices again, but now the two ghosts' conversation brought back that disturbing memory.

I never understood what Mr. Creepy and the little girl were talking about that night, but I knew it wasn't good. Obviously they wanted me to hear them: either the man wanted to scare me, or the brave little girl was letting me know that the man was threatening our family as well as her.

The Face Returns

The figure slowly materialized out of the black shadow of Jack's nightmare. Tall and menacing, it glided across the room until its face—or what was left of a face—loomed inches from Jack's eyeballs. Through the fog of his own cold, dripping sweat, Jack knew that this was not their first encounter. The spectral man was dressed to the nines in his usual attire, complete with a jet black silk top hat and cane, but this time his countenance resembled that of Max Schreck, the long-dead German silent film star of the eerie *Nosferatu*. Schreck always maintained that he was no actor; his stellar performance as a vampire was simply due to the fact that he was, in fact, a blood-sucking member of the Undead. As Jack stared up at the chilling chap that towered over him, he wondered if old Max had been right.

The figure's long bony fingers reached up toward its leering face and rested gently for a moment on either side of the cracked nose. Something not quite a smile stretched across the wide slit that passed for lips. Time crawled by as the wraith held Jack's terrified gaze captive. Suddenly, like a frenzied shark, the spirit tore through its own thin facial skin, its long nails digging deep into the holes where cheek cavities should have been. Twisting and tearing, the thing peeled off its own face, piece by piece. Gray fragments of its paper-thin flesh fluttered gently around Jack's hair in a halo and rested on his eyelashes and in the corners of his bone-dry mouth. Jack mentally braced himself for the putrid, rotting skull that would certainly emerge from under the masochist's torn flesh. What was actually exposed was much more frightening than mere bone.

It was the dripping demon face from the door.

Slimy gobs of luminous goo slid gracefully from its sagging eye sockets. Slowly, the demon's top lip slit rolled up like a cracked plastic window shade as the rest of its mouth dropped down, opening wider and wider until its jaw stretched down upon its chest like one long mass of melted wax. Salvadore Dali would have loved the sight. Suddenly the cavernous mouth erupted in a silent, ear-piercing scream that vibrated throughout the small room and tore straight into Jack's brain. He had to get away from that wail or go mad himself. Mustering his last ounce of energy, Jack forced his rubber legs to move his body back toward the sturdy rear wall and away from that muted shrieking thing. His eyes were glued to the demon's hypnotic glare. He couldn't even blink. There was only one thing that Jack could do to save himself: he had to make himself wake up. Defying the demon's paralyzing stare, Jack managed to shake his head from side to side, slowly at first, then with increasing ferocity. He imagined himself as a wild cat shaking off a clinging mouse. He dared not test his waning courage by admitting who actually was the hungry tiger and who was the half-eaten prey.

Suddenly, Jack's back hit something with a hard thud. His eyelids snapped shut; he had managed to shake himself awake out of bed and had hit the hard floor. Every bone in his back felt shattered by the impact, but pain never felt so good. Exhausted, Jack lay on the ground for several hours—or maybe it was just seconds—drinking in the safety of the cool darkness that his closed eyes offered. After a lifetime, he took a long, luscious breath and opened his eyes, savoring the expected sight of his bedroom's familiar white ceiling.

But Jack did not see heaven above. He saw hell. The demonic face still dripped and drooled inches from Jack's nose while its cavernous, cracked mouth continued the same silent, brain-screeching howl. Jack's back was not resting on the floor; it was pressed straight up against the cold plaster wall that he had backed into only moments ago. Jack had been awake the entire night. He had never gone to bed; he had been trapped in this room for longer than he could remember. His nightmare was not a dream, it was stark reality.

Jack sighed. "Here we go again ..."

Maybe my Scottish ancestors had the best solution:

From Ghoulies and Ghosties
and Long-Leggedy Beasties
and Things that go BUMP in the night,
Good Lord, deliver us!

The Cat with Nine Lives

Erin smiled as she felt the soft cat fur brush lightly against the right calf of her bare leg. She was dressing in her bedroom when the feline walked in through the door. The door had been shut and locked at the time, but Erin was quite used to all sorts of things drifting through our woodwork. This time, to her delight, her visitor was a nice black kitty.

The cat wrapped its tail lovingly around Erin's ankle, and then slowly disappeared from sight. Erin could still feel the purring against her leg. My excited daughter ran down the hall, burst into my room, and grabbed a funny old Christmastime photo that I kept on my dresser. It was of a black cat sitting in the middle of a holiday wreath, thoroughly disgusted that a large red velvet Santa hat had been stuck on her head.

"Mom, is this a picture of your cat, Black Magic?"

I wondered at my daughter's question. "You know it is. I've shown you that a million times. Poor kitty died a few years ago. She's buried in the backyard, right beside the bird bath and under a sweet little sign that says *Kitty Crossing*. Why?"

Erin pointed to the black feline in the photo. "This is the cat that I just saw in my bedroom!"

I was speechless. With the menagerie of ghosts that we had stomping around our house, Magic was the only one I had hoped to see but never did. Had my former pet chosen to visit my daughter, instead? Had she confused another little girl with me? Or had Erin confused my old pictures with her imagination?

My daughter was adamant. "Come into my room and see for yourself!"

"She's still in there?" I ran down the hall and stood in Erin's doorway. On the floor in front of the big white dresser was the shimmering shape of a cat. There was no doubt about it. The tail was held high, as cats do when they are enormously happy—or at least comfortably content. The feline slowly turned her head in my direction and then vanished.

Over the next few weeks, everyone in our family spotted Magic. She wandered through the front room as if she owned it and rubbed her luminous, dark fur against the leg of our dining room table. Her happy tail was always held straight up. One time, Jack insisted that he had seen a distinctly white cat, but our family's consensus was that Magic's iridescent fur had caught the light. For weeks, my black ghost cat drifted in and out of the corners of our eyes, but it was always and only Erin whom she visited in her cherished pink bedroom, which years before had been mine. I was admittedly a little jealous that Magic didn't spend quality time with me, but my pet's choice in appearing to Erin was natural: Magic had died only four months before Erin was born. I had always believed that Erin's birth was the balance of Magic's death, the same way that, four years later, Elise's birth had countered the passing of my dear ninety-eight-year-old grandfather. It was appropriate that these two souls should bond.

A few months later, as I stood in front of the stove scrambling a pan of eggs, I felt the soft side of a cat rub lovingly against my right calf, then it meandered forward until the tail hugged around my leg like an affectionate furry snake. *Purrpurrpurrrrr…* A bubble of happiness burst though me. I glanced down at my feet. The floor appeared empty, save for a few bread crumbs that had fallen from the toast I had just buttered. The cat turned around and brushed my leg again. I could feel every muscle in her small body ripple as she ran her smooth coat against my bare leg for a second time.

"Hi, Magic!"

I reached down to pet her, but, true to cat form, she scampered out of the kitchen and away. I didn't care— I had proof that my kitty hadn't forgotten about me after all!

That night a soft mewing drifted under my bedroom door from the hall. It wasn't the loud cry of a living animal; this sound emanated from a separate place between worlds. I knew who it was. Oh, how I wanted to open my door and scoop my little black cat into my arms, but I knew that was impossible. I'd heard phantom voices before and they always stopped when I stepped into the room. Instead, I sat on the floor, leaned my ear against the closed door, and savored every note from my far away friend.

Mew. Mewwwww…

I understood my Magic. She was saying good-bye to me. She hadn't had the chance to do so eight years ago when Jack drove her to the vet for the last time; she had been too ill and I had been too upset for farewells. I blinked back a tear. *Good-bye, my Huckleberry friend. I love you, too.*

A Gaggle of Ghosties:
Meet the Rest of our Spectral Menagerie!

The kind old man smiled through his swirling pipe smoke as two princesses, a witch, a mummy, a cheerleader, a very small vampire bride, and Robin Hood swarmed around the big wooden rocking chair with the plump blue pillows in which he relaxed. It was late October and our children's Halloween party was in full swing. Breathless from their neighborhood romp, the kids eagerly turned their black-and-orange buckets upside-down and dumped their goodies into one big gooey, crunchy lump in the middle of the coffee table. No one thought to share their treats with the sweet old man in the chair next to them. They couldn't see him. But Kristina could.

"Vivian, did you know that an old man with a gray crew cut and a pipe just walked through your front door?"

In any other household, such an announcement would be met with screams of terror, bottles of mace, and frantic phone calls to 911; in our house, it meant that we had another party-crashing ghost. I grabbed a frosty mug of Bloody Hand Punch, stuck a chocolate spider in my mouth, and squinted into the next room to catch a glimpse our latest ghostly guest. The elderly gentleman made himself right at home and had so much fun at our Halloween party that he returned for Christmas. Uninvited, of course.

Christmas evening brought a holiday-themed table overflowing with every goodie from Santa's snack sack. Great-grandma's china sparkled under the red and green lights of the massive evergreen that filled the air with the sweet smell of spruce. Tea cups tinkled and large glasses of scarlet-colored holiday punch spilled down thirsty throats and threatened silk shirts. Mrs. Wickham, ever the proper hostess, dutifully drifted from one laughing group to another, still incensed at being ignored but comforted that at least this time she knew what season we were celebrating.

"I see your spirits of Christmas Past have arrived!" my friend Nell laughed as I handed her a rum-soaked sugar plum. "Let's see, you've got one, two, three, four lined up against the far wall of the living room. Poor things. They're standing there staring at everyone like a bunch of confused wallflowers."

"*Four?*" I wondered how many of those alcoholic cookies my friend had eaten. "Nell, we only have three ghosts." I peered over the heads of my chattering guests. Four luminous forms stood with their backs against the wall, like a police lineup. Next to Mrs. Wickham stood our bad-tempered young lady with the dark hair, probably returning to tear up our Christmas stockings. And next to her stood—surprise, surprise—the nice little old man with the gray crew cut! He'd left his Halloween pipe at home and had brought a date instead—at least, I assumed the young woman standing next to him was his partner. I'd never seen her before. From the confused look on the old man's transparent face, I didn't think that he was quite sure who she was, either. I trotted back to Nell.

"More party crashers!" I giggled. "Who's that girl next to Mr. Crew Cut?"

Nell shrugged and gulped a glass of punch. "Never saw her before, but then, I don't live in your haunted house. Don't you know who she is?"

"Nope, and I don't care. This is Christmas. Good will to all, including ghosts!"

Four hours later, everyone had gone home except my friends Nell, Rose, Cammie, and the confused old man. His date had dumped him. Poor old guy. My friends and I collapsed onto the couches and began to munch on the few holiday cookies that still remained. While we happily chatted and chewed, the clueless old man started to wander slowly around the perimeter of the room. *Slowly* was an understatement; a rock could have beaten his pace. For the next hour, the ghost drifted across one side of the room, then squeezed around the corner and clung to the next. A slug could have left him in the dust. The old guy was so slow that we forgot all about him until he drifted into me. At first, the fingers on my left hand began to tingle. Then my left ear buzzed. My left eyebrow twitched. The little toe on my left foot went to sleep. Like a slow injection from the dentist before a tooth drill, the prickly feeling began to seep across the left side of my body and into my very center. The ghost moved right through me and never even knew I was there!

"I can't feel a thing!" I laughed. "This clueless guy is moving right through the space where I'm sitting. Even my eyelids feel numb!"

"Why don't you just get up and move?" Nell logically suggested as she stretched out over her end of the sofa.

"I don't want to upset him. He seems confused and a little sad. His date dumped him, you know. He might think that I'm rejecting him, too."

Rose, ever the skeptic, rolled her eyes. "Oh, for heaven's sake, Viv. You're probably numb because you haven't budged your bottom off that sofa for over an hour. Get up and do some jumping jacks!"

"Rose, my dear friend, Christmas is the time to practice charity, not aerobics!"

I think Mr. Crew Cut agreed.

My great-grandmother's antique china tea cup sat demurely on its matching saucer, propped in the center of the breakfast nook floor. Two feet to its right, two cupboard doors had been opened wide like a frantic mother trying to implore her wayward child to come in out of a busy street. The cupboard's fears were justified; at any time, five-year-old Elise could race through the room, her pink tennis shoes unconsciously aimed straight for a direct hit. The little 120-year-old cup would be reduced to a litter of bone china, scattered under the dining room table and into the yawning mouths of floor air vents.

Fortunately, I found it first.

"Alright, who's been going through my china?" I called out loud to the empty house. This was only a formality, of course, because I knew full well who the prodigal snoop was. I'd discovered our latest ghostly visitor the prior night when the sudden scent of her overly sweet perfume made me gag. It reminded me of how my grandmother's perfume bottles smelled the first time they were opened several years after the stale liquid inside had evaporated. At least Mrs. Wickham smelled of gardenia and jasmine and roses; this new ghostly dame had a yen for drug store cologne.

With my first whiff came the clear impression of its owner. She was eternally caught in that awkward age somewhere between teenager and adult. Her thick, dark blond hair hung loose over her shoulder, caught half up, half down with a large white satin bow, as was the fashion around the turn of the century. Her dress reflected the same time period: ankle-length, straight, but with a bit of a teasing flow, with a matching satin ribbon tied around her waist. She was about the same height as me. Either she wasn't aware of my presence, or she simply did not wish to acknowledge me.

I found her gazing at the china displayed in my formal glass cabinet that stood on public display at the foot of our stairway. She seemed to be genuinely attracted to my century-old plates and teacups. Then she turned and slowly began to wander, dream-like, into the kitchen before she melted away in its doorway. I didn't blame her sudden departure—my kitchen had not been cleaned and a few mountains of unwashed dishes still balanced perilously around the sink. I wanted to leave, too!

The next morning I discovered the wayward cup as I raced through the house frantically gathering my girls' dance outfits for their class, which had started ten minutes ago. It was another one of those days when I should have played hooky; I certainly didn't have time to play Sherlock Holmes. Erin, Elise, and even Savannah the cat were my suspects, but even if they dared to go through the china (which they never did), they would have to unlatch the hidden seventy-year-old cabinet locks that could only be opened with adult strength and a few pinched fingers. Not even kitty claws were that handy.

"I know you're here!" My threatening tone vibrated through the empty rooms. "No one touches my grandmother's china without permission. Keep your hands off or find another house to wander around!"

I never saw nor smelled the prim, pilfering young lady again and my teacups remained unmoved on their proper shelves. I often wonder if our neighbors' china is safe.

Four-year-old Max stared out into our empty living room.

"Mommy?"

He and the rest of his siblings, all of whom were friends with my daughters, were visiting us for "home movie night." This outing didn't involve long drives to a movie theatre or expensive tickets, it was the result of one quick trip to the video store and a fun evening gathered together in front of our VCR with a lot of pizza. Tonight's feature was the classic *National Velvet*. All the horse-loving kids sat mesmerized as little Elizabeth Taylor's horse streaked past the other galloping goofs. Max had never taken his eyes once from the TV screen. All at once, he had hopped up, thrown open the door, and started off at a fast trot straight for our empty front room.

"Max, where are you going?" I was the only adult and in charge of my friend's children, as well as my own. Still facing the front room, little Max looked over his shoulder at me. His face was one big question mark.

"Where's Mommy?" he asked.

"Mommy's at your house. You know that. I'm going to drive all you guys home as soon as the movie is over."

Max was adamant. "No! No! Mommy's here. I heard her. She called me. 'Max! Max!' she said. I have to go to Mommy!"

Now I was scared. I didn't doubt Max's words one bit, but this was the first time that one of our ghosts had actually spoken to someone who was not an immediate member of my family. And of all people, they had picked on innocent little Max.

I grabbed Matt's hand and firmly steered him back to his place in front of the TV set. "No, Max, Mommy's not here. Just sit and watch the movie. It's almost over, then I'll take you home."

"No, Mommy called me! Mommy..." The confused little boy was near tears.

I locked the door firmly behind me and handed him a second dish of ice cream. Max instantly cheered up and forgot all about the female voice that he'd heard. Thanks to Max, I had now discovered two sure ways to combat ghosts: prayer and a second dish of ice cream.

Erin's screams shook the house. She was ballistic—terrified beyond description. I bolted from the kitchen where I'd been cutting up vegetables for dinner's soup and raced up the staircase in five leaps. My eight-year-old daughter was already halfway down the same steps. Her face was pure white with horror; her sea-blue eyes bulged with naked fear. I feared she was close to shock.

"Erin, sweetheart, what's wrong? What happened?" I reached out to hug her. For the first time in her entire life, my daughter pulled away as if I was a stranger.

"Why did you scream at me?" she wailed from the top step. "Why? What did I do? I was just sitting in my room and you *screamed*..."

"Erin, honey, I didn't make a sound. I was downstairs in the kitchen."

"...you screamed at me from the stairway! You yelled my name so mean! You screamed *Erin Campbell-Miller*!"

I ran up the rest of the stairs between us and grabbed my trembling daughter's shoulders. "Erin, calm down and think. Just now you stood on this stairway and saw me run out of the kitchen and up the steps. How could I yell at you from the stairway if I was in the kitchen?"

A faint spark of recognition flickered in Erin's red eyes. She threw her arms around my neck and burst into a second flood of hot tears. We collapsed on the top landing together.

"Did you fall asleep in your room, sweet pea? Did you have a little nap that ended up with a real-sounding nightmare?"

Erin was incensed. "I was wide awake! Do I look like I just woke up?" She was right. I'd even heard the sounds of her playing in her room. At least, I assumed it was Erin.

"Well, maybe it was a lady out in the street yelling at her child," I offered hopefully.

"Mom, nobody's outside right now. And it was *my* name."

I was out of lucid suggestions. My daughter demanded one. I refused to claim that her eyes and ears "playing tricks" on her as my mother did when I had ghost experiences as a child. I gulped, said a short silent prayer, and began:

"Sweetie, there's only one other thing I can think of. You know that we have some ghosts in this house sometimes, right? You remember my nice kitty, Black Magic, and you've heard that little girl calling to me. Well, I think that a mean ghost might have drifted in here and yelled just to scare you."

Erin looked up at me with big, trusting eyes. *Oh please, God, don't let me say something that will scare her.* I continued:

"You know that I have never and would never yell at you like that, right?"

Erin nodded her head. She'd never been frightened of me. I'd always been her protector.

"Let's bow our heads and ask God to make that grumpy ghost leave our house for good."

Afterward, Erin trotted back up to her room with a grin as wide as can be.

On a cold Friday afternoon one week before Thanksgiving and one day before my parents' fifty-first wedding anniversary, my mother died unexpectedly. I couldn't bear to tell my two little girls, and I decided that the bitter news could wait until Monday. That same surreal night, I left the rest of my family at the local school carnival and escaped alone to our house—the same home where Mama had grown up and then raised me. I stood in my front yard, bathed only in the callous yellow beam of our single streetlight, wondering what right the rest of the unfeeling world had to go on acting as if this was just another day. Shock oozed through my veins, dripped from my pores, and clotted my brain. Nothing looked quite right. The moon was the wrong color. The sky was dark, and the big house in front of me was darker. There may have been stars, but I didn't see them. Everything vanished except one of the few members of my family still left on this Earth with me: my home.

The old building's despondency mirrored my broken heart. The kind old oaks stretched their craggy limbs over the gray roof in a black silhouette of lace, creating a mourning shroud. I couldn't bear to walk inside the front door; doing so would disturb its grief. Instead, I wandered into our unlit backyard, long ago tamed from the wild jungle that it once was, and stood quietly in the place that I had created to renew my spirit: my small peace lily garden. It was comfortably nestled beneath the watchful eye of our breakfast nook window. Dozens of milky blossoms, iridescent under the moonlight, waved their leaves as they danced around my grandmother Mary's sixty-three-year-old sky blue tiled bird bath. A red blossom nestled in the far back crook of the cozy plot marked the final resting place of my best feline friend, Black Magic. This was my Nirvana, the private retreat that I embraced when my tired soul needed to restore its serenity and peace. That night, my little garden also became my mother's memorial place. My memory danced back to an old Scottish song she used to sing to me:

> *Will ye no come back again?*
> *Will ye no come back again?*
> *Better would ye canna be,*
> *Will ye no come back again?*

"Well, she's gone," I whispered to the gloom. I looked up to the house, but only the empty windows returned my gaze. There were no ghosts. This was a private funeral. It was time to add my precious mother's name to the house's long and honored legacy. In the silent darkness, the old house seemed to wrap its solid strength around me as we struggled together to say good-bye to Mama.

Our lives were never the same after that night. My two little girls and I struggled to regain perspective. Pre-teen Erin, who had been especially close to her grandmother, fell into the deepest despair and took to sleeping with Mama's thick yellow sweater wrapped around her every night. "It feels like Grandma's arms are still hugging me," she would whisper during our good-night kisses. By daylight, I managed to don my "brave parent" mask, never failing to stay positive and rain smiles on my grieving children; I cried by myself at night until my eyes were swollen shut, and then I cried some more. Getting through each day became an effort. Breathing was painful. We knew that Mama was out of pain and in perfect peace, but we selfishly longed for just one more laugh, one more twinkle from her sparkling black eyes, one more hug from her loving arms—one more *anything*. We refused to remember how osteoporosis had hacked and twisted her back into a deep, gruesome S, crippling her so terribly that she could barely pull herself across the floor on her walker. We closed our minds to the years of gagging, coughing attacks that threatened to steal her every breath while she frantically gasped for air. We just wanted Mama and Grandma back with us. Thank goodness that God knew better than we did. We never heard from Mama again after her death, and that's become my biggest comfort. It means she's at peace.

After four bleak months, our iceberg of despair finally began to crack with the first warm kiss of springtime. My father agreed to move in with us in the family homestead. The apartment he had shared with my mom for the past twelve years had become cold and meaningless without her smiles. Our house, on the other hand, was still very much alive with the din of laughing children and the everyday hustle and bustle of life—not to mention our boisterous phantoms. The house had not died with Mama; it had simply gathered her memory into its history. Every morning the sun still shone through the big bedroom window on the top floor. The same family of blue jays continued to hop around Grandma Mary's stone birdbath in the backyard. Five-year-old Elise still curled up in the velvet lap of her great-great-grandmother's hand-carved loveseat. This had been my dad's adopted home even when it still belonged to my maternal grandparents: he was married under the alcove in the front room; his daughter and grandchildren were raised here; his beloved in-laws had died here. We all agreed that rather than have Daddy continue to live alone in his tiny apartment, he should move in with us. We needed him. He needed us. The house needed everyone. God had given us the perfect place to heal together.

Daddy's anticipated arrival prompted yet another round of room renovation. The bedroom at the end of the upstairs hallway was, for the third time, scraped and repainted for another inhabitant. True, during the last few

years it had earned a reputation as being one of the favorite hang-outs of our spooks, but my father was decid-
edly not ghost-sensitive. I had no fear of his sleep being
disturbed in there, as had my poor mother-in-law's a decade before. The boldest spook's bravado would whither
when faced with my stubborn dad. Despite the past unexplained escapades with his hide-and-go-seek cell phone,
Daddy adamantly did not believe in ghosts. Period. That
attitude alone made him a prime target for our ghosts'
pranks, and they wasted no time getting started on him
after he moved in. I tried to warn him, but he wouldn't
believe it...

Daddy's eyes flew open. In all his eighty years, he had
never heard such a racket! The mournful chorus of deep,
Scottish voices bellowed imploringly from the depths
of his upstairs bedroom. He squinted at the green LCD
numbers glowing on the clock-radio next to him. It was
after one in the morning! Logic would assume that my
insomniac father had once again misplaced his hearing
aids while listening to some of his favorite Scottish bedtime music. The problem was that Daddy wasn't in his
upstairs bedroom. He had fallen asleep downstairs in his
armchair and hadn't stepped a foot upstairs since before
dinner that evening.

Although Daddy was absolutely delighted with his
newly renovated bedroom, he spent most of his time immersed in his study on the first floor. This was the same

room that, forty-three years ago, had been added to the house as my ailing grandmother's bedchamber, then it was passed on to centurion missionary Aunt Grace, then on to Jack and me until Erin and Elise threw us out and made it into their giant playroom. One month before my father's arrival, the girls' toys were hauled upstairs and the ground floor room was repainted a crisp white with a brand-new wall-to-wall marine-blue shag carpet, which mercifully covered the four decades of stains embedded on the cracked bare wood floor. Daddy, known to his grandchildren as Poppy, approved the entire renovation and promptly moved in his complete living room set and home office furniture. Elise dubbed the gleaming transformation Poppy's Playroom, in honor of her grandfather, and it was everyone's favorite room in the house. Especially Poppy!

Sleep was rarely on my dad's nocturnal menu. After supper, he preferred to digest his late-night bowls of buttered popcorn and Tootsie-Roll pops from the comfort of his cozy downstairs study, stretched out in his enormous velveteen armchair with his bare toes happily wiggling in front of a brand-new 30-inch widescreen TV. He rarely trudged up the stairs to his own bed before two in the morning; three thirty was his normal bedtime. Tonight was an early evening for night-owl Daddy: it was only one thirty, but that darned music roaring down from his upstairs bedroom had rudely disturbed his midnight nap. Daddy always fell asleep the moment that he switched on his TV, and his snores were dwarfed only by CNN's ear-splitting drone. Daddy disliked hearing aids and delighted in regularly "losing" his own expensive pair. He found it much easier to simply turn the volume full blast on everything else rather than futz with sticking things in his ears. Apparently, tonight he had forgotten to switch off his bedroom radio before coming downstairs to eat dinner. The funny thing was that Daddy was sure he hadn't listened to any music in that room at all that day.

My irritated father charged up the creaky old staircase to confront the Celtic din that wailed from his empty bedroom. Even without his trusty hearing aids, he could plainly hear the bagpipes wail the next wailing ballad.

My father flung open his bedroom door and peered into the pitch-black shadows. In the far back corner, just to the left of his small white sofa and my great-grandmother's jade floor lamp, glowed one small red eye. He knew that eye. He had seen it staring eerily, unblinking, from that same corner many times since he moved in. He never mentioned it to anyone because he knew exactly what it meant: his CD player was on. Undoubtedly, his granddaughters had been playing with his stereo. At least they had the good taste to pick out one of his favorite Scottish ballads. The real mystery was how the rest of our family could sleep while the entire building shook with bagpipes and guitars and flutes and a chorus of disembodied baritone Scotsmen belching forth yet another endless chorus of Celtic complaints.

Daddy switched on the light and switched off his screaming stereo. *How could Vivian sleep through that racket?* he wondered again to himself. *She's in the next room! Why didn't she just come in here and turn it off?*

The next morning at breakfast, Daddy was full of apologies.

"I'm sorry about my music playing so loudly last night! I guess I forgot that I'd put it on when I went downstairs to dinner. I wish you'd just turned it off for me instead of enduring it for so long. Did the girls get to sleep at all?"

I stared blankly at my father. "What music?"

Daddy returned my surprised expression. "When I came upstairs late last night, my bedroom stereo was playing at full blast. You must have heard it. My ears ached from the racket, and I didn't even have my hearing aids in!"

I looked across the breakfast table at my father. "Daddy, I didn't hear a thing. You know very well that I'm the lightest sleeper in this house. I can tell exactly who is walking in our front door or up our stairs when I'm in bed with my door shut. I wake up when I hear you get up in the middle of the night and sit in that big, squeaky leather chair by your bed. In fact, I can tell you what time you came upstairs last night: it was around one thirty, right? I heard you walk into your room, and then you went back into the hall and in the bathroom ..."

My father was dumbfounded. "That's impossible! You sleep in the room right next to mine! I know I wasn't imagining this, because the door was literally shaking from the music's vibrations when I pushed it open." He turned toward his young granddaughters, who were obediently munching their waffles next to him. "Didn't you girls hear anything last night?"

"No, Poppy." They looked as confused as I did.

My father was unabashed. "Come on, you guys, stop playing around. You heard that music, right? Your mommy just told you not to say anything to me so you could play a trick on me, right?"

I was insulted. "Daddy! You know very well I would never tell any of my children to lie to you or to anyone else, not to mention that we've never played a single prank on you in our entire lives! Why would we turn up your stereo in the middle of the night and then pretend to be asleep, especially on a school night?"

Just then, Ian innocently walked in and reached for the cereal box.

"Ian, did you hear any music late last night?"

My twenty-year-old stepson glanced up suspiciously from his breakfast bowl. "Uh...no. No *music*. But I did hear voices in Poppy's room. It was after midnight sometime. I came home late from the movies and saw the light shining from beneath his door, so I was going to knock and say good-night, but then I heard those voices. I thought he was on the phone, except that nobody sounded like Poppy and—this is the really weird part—they had Scottish accents! I finally decided that Poppy must be talking on his speaker phone to one of his friends in Scotland. You know, that difference in international time would make sense why he would be talking so late. Anyway, I went into the bathroom and when I came out again, the light was out in Poppy's room and everything was quiet, so I figured that he had gone to sleep. I wasn't in the bathroom more than a few minutes, but you know how fast Poppy falls asleep sometimes."

My father stared in disbelief Ian's words. "Well, now I've heard everything. Even my grandson is in on this trick! You know very well that I don't have a speaker-phone. I wasn't even upstairs before one thirty!"

Ian grinned and stuffed a waffle in his mouth. He knew this house too well to be surprised by anything.

Poor Daddy never accepted the simple fact that as long as he snubbed our resident spirits, he would remain irresistible bait for them. He had a logical explanation for every illogical situation. Sometimes he was right, but most of the time he just rolled his eyes. Finally, on a lazy Saturday afternoon in late June, skeptical Daddy met his match.

The Normandy veteran had spent the month of June 2004 traveling around the countries that the Second World War had led him to in his youth: France, England, and especially his beloved motherland, Scotland. He returned home from the Highlands with tales of heather-covered castles older than America, lost bed-and-breakfasts surrounded by shaggy sheep and cattle, and endless greetings from our Scots cousins. His favorite discovery popped up in the middle of a Highland town so small that most maps forgot about it. In the middle of this enchanting village he happened upon the John Buchan Study Center. This Scottish author was remembered primarily for his mystery novel *The Thirty-Nine Steps*, which was made famous in the 1930s by film director Alfred Hitchcock. Buchan's museum piqued Daddy's interest to read more of the Scotsmans' works.

"Vivian, don't we have some old books around here by John Buchan?" My father sat in the middle of our home's library, surrounded by piles of assorted volumes as he methodically searched for Buchan's elusive novels.

"I never heard of the man," I confessed with some embarrassment. "Bookworm" was practically my middle name but, despite the fact that English literature had been one of my major studies in college, I was constantly reminded that I was not as well-read as I imagined myself to be.

Dust billowed gracefully as my father threw another book on the pile. "Your grandmother's cousin sent some of Buchan's books to her from Scotland a long time ago. I remember looking through them when Granddaddy Hosie lived here."

"For heaven's sake, Daddy, that was over forty years ago! I've cleaned and re-shelved every single book in this entire house. These books are so well-organized—or, at least, they were before you started rearranging them—

that I can tell you exactly where every title is located. Believe me, there are no books by John Buchan."

My father pulled one last book off the wooden shelf and sighed. "I'm going out to grab a cup of coffee. I need a break. If you see those books ..."

"...I'll set them aside for you." My dad and I often finished each other's sentences. We knew each other that well.

I wandered upstairs to finish folding another heap of clean laundry. Erin and Elise played a board game on the floor beside me. The house was quiet; the downstairs was empty. Thirty minutes later, the house shook as the front door slammed shut with an explosive BAM! Poppy had returned home from the coffee shop.

"Hey, Vivian! Thanks for finding these!" My elated father waved three small, water-stained red books through my open doorway. I paused over my piles of terrycloth towels and peered at the texts. Despite the fact that their pages had faded from white to crusty brown decades before I was born, they were still in fairly good condition. Scarlet cloth decorated the covers, with the initials "J. B." proudly displayed in the midst of a striking gold emblem. Gingerly, I picked up the first volume and glanced at its title: *Prester John* by John Buchan.

"Daddy, I've never seen any of these books in my life." Astounded, I carefully opened to the inside cover. The handwritten inscription confirmed my instincts about its age:

To
Mary
from
Cousin John

With all good wishes
Sept. 1926

"Where on earth did you find these?" I asked. "Did you drive over to that used bookstore in Winter Park?"

My father raised his eyebrows in question. "I only went down the street to Starbucks. They don't even have magazines there. Didn't *you* find them? They were waiting for me on the dining room table in the library when I walked in the front door. I thought that you put them there for me."

Eavesdropping Erin chimed in the conversation. "But, Poppy! Mommy has been folding laundry upstairs all day!" I couldn't help bursting into laughter. Another one of our friendly spirits was "helping" my dad again. I had a good suspicion of the culprit, but I wasn't going to breathe one syllable of the name to my family.

"Daddy, take my word for it, just walk back to the library, say *Thank you very much* in a nice, loud voice, then find a big, comfy chair and enjoy your books."

My father shook his head. "I'll read these books alright, but I'm not saying another single word about how they appeared on that table."

And he never did.

Erin lay in her bed, happily watching the first stray beams of sunshine wink through the closed cotton curtains and dance among the folds of the white down comforter that had hugged her warmly all through the cool March night. The quiet of the early morning was absolute. Not even the resident blue jay was awake yet. Nothing in the entire house moved except for a few timid sunbeams on her blanket and the rainbow of spirit orbs that chased each other in and out of the lath and plaster walls on the far side of her bedroom. These were the first to wish Erin a happy eleventh birthday.

She hadn't noticed the orbs at first. The sunbeams were mesmerizing enough, and she had been lost in her thoughts of today's birthday events: a morning of horseback riding followed by a shopping spree with Mom and an afternoon of dancing with friends and cupcakes covered with purple icing and rainbow sprinkles. Her party had been celebrated yesterday, since her real birthday, which was today, fell on a Monday when most kids were in school. But not Erin. Not today. Mountains of presents and cards and other endless party remnants from yesterday's party guests were packed around Erin's bed and seemed to stretch from wall to wall. Her floor was practically impassible. It was a good thing that those orbs could fly.

The orbs were a surprising beginning to Erin's birthday morning, but not entirely unexpected. After all, the theme of Sunday's birthday party had been Harry Potter. It had been a logical choice for this particular birthday, since in the book, age eleven was the first year in which blossoming wizards and witches were invited (by owl telegram) to attend the prestigious Hogwarts School of Witchcraft and Wizardry. Orange cardboard boxes and black plastic crates of Halloween decorations had been dragged out of storage eight months early; the rooms were filled with blazing black candles, smoking cauldrons of green punch, and a gaggle of grinning bats, witches, spell books, and magic wands in an effort to transform our old haunted house into Harry's alma mater. Every child—and a few parents—had arrived dressed as a character or beast from the famous book series. One little boy even managed to transform himself into the 9¾ train platform that led to the wizards' academy! Spells of baking soda and vinegar bubbled out of their pots and all over the front sidewalk. Grade-school Muggles took a solemn oath to remain wizards and witches for the rest of their lives. "Flying" brooms nearly decapitated those who did not pay attention.

Erin's magical party roared on long after sunset, until candlelight and the full moon became the only sources of light. At three minutes past midnight, Erin drifted from age ten to age eleven. With a party like that, it was amazing that only a few orbs dropped in. We supposed that our other resident ghosts were on spring break while we celebrated Halloween in the middle of March. But what else would you do in a haunted house?

The first orb to greet Erin was pure white, like a smaller version of the full moon that had bathed her midnight birthday party. There was no mistaking it for a sunbeam. Sunbeams were tiny, delicate fairies; spirit orbs were a rainbow of glowing snowballs. Erin saw it whisk straight out of the ceiling above the entrance to her closet, then disappear just as quickly straight through the closed door that led to the hallway. Before she had time to catch her breath, a second and third orb, both white, popped into her bedroom from the same spot in the ceiling and drifted slowly around. Erin said that this placid duo reminded her of "a mother and her child taking a nice stroll in the park." Suddenly, a brilliant green orb appeared and flashed past the meandering white pair, disrupting their calm constitutional. They disappeared in its milky wake through the bedroom door. Erin considered following them, but she knew that even if she could make her way through the mass of birthday toys and games, the orbs would most likely have gone on their way by the time she reached the hallway. It was easier to stay snuggled in her bed with the sunbeams.

For several minutes, Erin lay motionless on her pillow, contemplating the mystical performance she had just witnessed. Suddenly, the green orb, which had grown to the size of a pie plate, burst through her ceiling, whirled in an emerald frenzy past her pile of birthday presents, and shot straight through the closed door like the grand finale of a fireworks display. It was wonderful.

Erin smiled. "Happy birthday to me!"

The ghosts in our house are familiar to us, yet they are not the spirits of any family member that I know of. I've said I'm glad that my mother has not appeared to me, because that means she is at peace—but that doesn't mean I've never longed for one last good-bye with a loved one. A few years after we moved into the great old house, I got that unique chance at a carnival, of all places ...

Any pet dog will tell you that every person has their own distinct scent. Sometimes those scents have a name: my best friend's mom always smelled of vanilla, and my next door neighbor, rescuer of lost animals, smelled of dog food. I reek of coffee. But, sometimes there is no word to describe an individual's scent. You just know that smell. It waltzes around their house or sticks to their favorite sweater. It can pop out of their open pocketbook or drift out of their pillow, but when you smell it, you see their face.

One Fourth of July, my grandfather came back on the summer breeze.

"Mommy! I wanna face paint!" Four-year-old Erin's tiny hand grabbed mine and pulled me toward a mile-long line of hyperactive preschoolers and sunburned parents. We would be stuck there for an hour.

"Erin, wouldn't you rather play in the bounce house again? Or maybe have another piece of watermelon? Those lines are shorter ..."

Erin gave me "the look." Every parent knows "the look." Sometimes it can, and should, be ignored, but never, ever in the middle of a Fourth of July celebration surrounded by free hot dogs and laughing families and everyone singing "You're A Grand Old Flag" as they wave to the Amtrak train rumbling by. I sighed and obediently took my place behind the fifty-second child who was patriotically waiting to have his face decorated.

While Erin made new friends in the endless line, I turned my face up to the clouds. I needed a Fourth of July like this. One year ago, on this very day, my beloved grandfather had passed away quietly in a darkened room at the end of a hall in a nursing home. He was four months shy of his ninety-ninth birthday and three months short of the birth of his second great-grandchild. Saying goodbye to the man who had gallantly escorted me to my haunted college dorm was very difficult. He was one of my very favorite people in the world. I missed him more than I would have missed chocolate.

I smiled, closed my eyes, and took a deep breath of warm summer air.

The smell of hot dogs and face paint vanished. I smelled Granddaddy. There was no mistaking it. That was his scent—sort of woodsy and musty. I knew that as long as I breathed in, that smell would stay with me, but the moment that I released this one breath, my grandfather would be gone. My eyes popped open. I stared, unblinking, at a single cloud. The summer sky had frozen. The heavens held its breath with me.

I could feel him. Not standing beside me; I was still surrounded by giggling, paint-spattered kids and empty potato chip bags. Granddaddy was way, way above me, somewhere in that amazing blue sky, smiling down and enveloping me with all of the love that we had shared in our three decades together. We were joined by this one breath.

I'm so proud of you, Viv. My heart heard his words as distinctly as if he was whispering in my ear. *Don't cry. I'm in ultimate joy. Keep living your life just like you are. I love you so, so much.*

I continued to inhale, slowly, slowly, pulling my grandfather closer. My overstuffed lungs were ready to pop. They screamed for relief, but I wouldn't budge. This breath was my last link with Granddaddy. Nothing else mattered.

Just one more second, I pleaded with my lungs. *I can't let him leave. Not just yet.*

The time had come to say goodbye. I had to let my Granddaddy go again. I wasn't releasing him like a dove into heaven; he had made that trip a year ago all by himself. No, it was my grief that he was taking, and he replaced it with his deep, unending love for me. That was far easier to carry for the rest of my life.

Slowly, slowly, I breathed out, releasing that magical air back into the atmosphere. I could feel my grandfather fading. My eyes filled with tears. The woman standing next to me assumed that I had been staring at the sun for too long.

"Good-bye, Granddaddy," I whispered. "I love you."

I turned my head back to the ground and gazed at my little daughter, who was still bubbling with excitement toward the face painting booth. "Mommy, we've taken a big step forward!"

I smiled. "Yes, we have, sweetie. More than you know." I glanced up one more time. The clouds just floated on by.

seven

Ghosts and
Girl Scouts

Ocala National Forest, Florida:
Spring 2007

These woods are full of werewolves!"
A gaggle of hyperactive early-teenage Girl Scouts, all drunk on the lack of bedtime, stuck their heads out of my van's windows and howled in delighted terror. The sun had set on the Ocala National Forest four hours ago, draining the woods of all color and morphing the tangled trees into one solid, black mass. My ancient, overstuffed Chevy van rumbled and stumbled along the narrow dirt

road, which was pockmarked with potholes that made it look like the site of a meteor shower. The surrounding darkness was claustrophobic; our world extended only as far as the pale yellow beams from the headlights could reach. I had been the troop leader of Erin's Girl Scout troop for over seven years, but never before had I led my girls into a place like this!

"Sandy swore the cabin was right here!" My friend and fearless assistant troop leader, Diane, sat in the left passenger seat and squinted down at a rumpled, hand-drawn map balanced between her knees. When Diane's friend had offered our Girl Scout troop a free weekend at her cabin in the woods, we thought our dream had come true; now we were stuck in the middle of a bad horror flick. It was ten minutes to midnight, my gas gauge was kissing E, and we were lost in the middle of a haunted forest.

"You know, they say that the ghosts of Indians still roam here," Sally sweetly informed her frightened friends, who were huddled beside her in the rear bench seat. "They died because of the white people, so now they wreak their revenge on all non-Indian people who dare to come in here at night!"

"They can't hurt *me*!" Molly shouted. "I'm Indian!"

Diane rolled her eyes at her daughter. "Molly, you're not American Indian; Dad is from the West Indies."

I had become numb to such inane conversations hours ago. My mind was lost in a game of Find the Cabin. "I wish I had room to at least turn the van around," I complained as I wheeled around another gaping pothole. "This stupid road is hardly wide enough for a person to walk!"

"That's because these are all old Indian trails!" sinister Sally hissed. "Oh…my…gosh! Wh—what is that up ahead? It…it looks like…"

"Cabin, ho!" Eleven-year-old Kaley suddenly sang out as she thrust her pointer finger through the front seat. "See it? See it, Miss Vivian? Right there!"

The van lurched over a craggy hill and bottomed out beside a rusty mailbox perched on top of a splintered wooden stake. To the right of the mailbox flowed an open space of land with a small, one-story wooden cottage hidden at the far end of the shadows. Its red roof caught the glint of moonlight reflected off the lake beyond. Diane jumped out of the van and was halfway to the front porch before I had time to set the parking brake. Every ancient American Indian spirit scrambled for safety in her nononsense wake. Half a blink later, twelve green-vested and shouting little girls joined her.

"Where's the porch light switch?" I heard Diane grumble from the depth of the darkened front steps. "Sandy said it was right by the door—"

Pop! A friendly lemon-colored light bulb blinked on above a small "Welcome, Friends!" sign that hung just beside the doorbell.

"You found it just in time!" I laughed to my friend.

"Well, somebody found it," Diane admitted. "I don't see a switch anywhere here. Do you kids see a switch?"

"All I see are mosquitoes!" wailed Lori. "My arm is bleeding from them! Miss Vivian, I'm allergic to bugs!"

Diane shoved the girls into the cabin and shut the mosquitoes out. An hour later, our overstuffed van had been unloaded and everyone had made the comfy little cabin into our troop home for the weekend. Most of the girls slung their sleeping bags over the array of sofas and chairs in the "great room," while the remaining scouts snuggled around the old brick fireplace in the adjoining sitting room, which was stuffed with six mismatched rockers and an old phonograph. Diane and I, the only adults of the group, took full advantage of our seniority by grabbing the only two bedrooms (and beds) for ourselves. Only my younger daughter, six-year-old Elise, who wasn't even a member of the troop, was allowed to share my room; all the other girls slept on the floor or on a stolen part of a couch. This was camping at its best!

Several mugs of hot chocolate and board games later, everyone finally climbed into their assorted sleeping places. I heard the last girl start to snore around two in the morning.

Stomp! Stomp! Stomp!

Diane opened one eye and peered into the pitch blackness of her bedroom. She was too exhausted to bother lifting her head from her pillow, but there was no need. She knew who the intruder was.

"Molly!" she whispered to her daughter through the dark, "What the heck do you think you're doing walking in here? No, you may *not* sleep with me. You just march right back out there and sleep where you're supposed to!"

The footsteps paused beside her bed and seemed to consider the command. Diane was in no mood for middle-of-the-night negotiations. She raised her head six inches from her feather pillow and said, "I'm warning you, young lady! Don't you make me get out of this warm bed!"

That last threat seemed to do the trick: a moment later, Diane heard the footfalls, softer now, quietly melt into the outer room. She wondered why she hadn't heard Molly open the door. Or shut it.

In the next room, Erin raised her sleepy head from her pillow, which was squashed between Bree, on her left, and Molly, on her right. What was Miss Diane yelling about? Molly wasn't in that bedroom; she was snoring right in Erin's ear! *I wish Miss Diane wouldn't talk so loudly in her sleep*, Erin frowned to herself in the darkness. *I wish Molly would get her sleeping bag out of that empty fireplace, too!* Erin plopped back onto her own pillow and closed her eyes.

"Erin. Erin, is that you?"

Erin sat up for the second time, this time focusing in the dark toward my voice that came from behind the closed bedroom door.

I had first mistaken the footsteps at the foot of my bed for Elise toddling off to the bathroom, until I glanced to my right and saw my younger daughter still snuggled next to me, deep in undisturbed sleep. The footfalls were unmistakable; I could hear them quite plainly walking around the foot of our double bed. At Elise's insistence, I had left the bedside lamp burning brightly, but I still couldn't see who was making loud footsteps! I concluded to myself it was Erin. *She's sleep walking again and probably fell asleep on the floor where I can't see her.* I pushed back the thick patchwork quilt, crawled to the far end of the bed and hung my head over the edge. No Erin. No anyone.

Stomp! Stomp!

The footsteps practically tromped over my upside down ears! I popped my head back upright from the floor, sat on my knees in the center of the bed, and stared around the brightly lit room. Suddenly, I saw her—but not with my eyes. She was an older lady, dressed in a blue, knee-length dress that reflected the modest fashion of an everyday middle class woman from the 1940s. Loose, thick finger waves rolled over her dark, short hair. She lived here. This was her home. She quietly wandered these rooms every single night, content in her safe, private world. Tonight, however, she was irritated and perturbed; who were all these strange people in "her" beds and why were all these little girls sleeping all over "her" furniture and floors? Rude strangers and interlopers were not to be tolerated!

"Get out of here!" I whispered loudly at the woman. "We're trying to sleep and you're gonna wake everybody up with all that noise! Stop stomping and go away!"

The woman vanished.

I lay back in bed and pulled the jostled blanket back over sleeping Elise's shivering little body. I sighed. So, there was a ghost in here after all. I had my suspicions when I first saw the silhouette of the cabin peek out of the moonlight and felt the unsettling "buzz" of paranormal energy. Every single digital photo that I had taken of the girls that evening was riddled with orbs. I desperately wanted them to be dust specks, or dew drips, but no such luck. They were rainbow-colored energy orbs, all bouncing merrily in-between and around the heads of our unsuspecting troop. I had kept my mouth shut about the spooks, never suspecting that the haunting would become so personally interactive! Oh, great. We were stuck with a grumpy ghost for the weekend.

I slipped out of bed, tiptoed to my bedroom door, and peeked out at the girls in the outer rooms. No stomps; only snores. Even Erin seemed to be fast asleep. Good. Grumpy Grandma Ghost had only awakened me, which wasn't surprising since I was a light sleeper, like many parents. I returned to my bed, kissed my sleeping child, and wondered what the heck I was going to do with that ghost.

The sun rose bright and happy the next morning and never stopped smiling 'til the moon shoved it back over the edge of the horizon. We burned blueberry pancakes in the kitchen, found small animal skulls down by the sparkling lake, and explored meandering trails that drifted from paw print to paw print. The Ocala National Forest was an enchanted woodland during daylight. Cardinals sung from the cloud tops and everyone made pine needle necklaces. More orbs popped up in my photos...or maybe they were just sun spots. *Yeah*, I thought. *That was it. Just sun spots.*

Later that night we were again faced with the raw exposure of bedtime. Molly looked at her mother in complete confusion as she was strictly admonished not to step one toe out of her sleeping bag all night. I was tempted to defend the innocent scout by explaining our ghostly visitor to Diane, but I decided to keep quiet on the subject. I didn't want to give our phantom hostess any ideas about an encore.

The girls' next morning breakfast debate was about whether twelve-year-old Bonnie was a vivid dreamer or a crazy liar. "I tell you, I saw a big Indian man staring in at us from the outside of the glass doors last night!" she insisted to her sister scouts over pancakes and bacon. "He was glaring down at us, like he wanted to scalp us!"

"Nuh-uh!" Molly rolled her eyes at her friend. "You were just dreaming, Bonnie. Sally scared you with her Indian ghost stories."

"We told stories about werewolves, too," Bonnie argued, "so why didn't I dream about them, huh? I'm telling you, I was the only one awake and the moonlight was lighting him up. He had an axe with a big stone on the end, too!"

"You saw the moonlight," Carol laughed. "If you were so sure it was a ghost come to scalp us, how come you didn't wake everybody up?"

"I was too scared!" Bonnie wailed. "I'm glad we're leaving today. I don't think the ghosts like us being here."

"Well, my friend Miss Sandy sure likes us being here or she wouldn't have invited us." Diane smiled as she placed a pile of steaming biscuits in the middle of the dining table. "She's the very-much-alive owner of this lovely cabin, and no matter if you believe in ghosts or not, she's the one who has the final say."

By the time that the last piece of toast had been buttered, the troop members agreed that the cabin was undoubtedly haunted *and* was the most wonderful place we had every stayed. The girls couldn't wait to get back home, *and* they couldn't wait to come back to the cabin as soon as Miss Sandy would let them.

At five minutes past one that afternoon, every last suitcase and pillow and Girl Scout was packed in my van. Our girls had truly earned their cleaning badges (if there had been such a thing!); the snug cabin shone brighter than when we had first stepped inside two nights prior. "Leave the place cleaner than we found it," was always one of our troop mottos.

I leaned against the open breakfast bar that separated the narrow kitchen from the rest of the great room as I waited for Diane to finish a second cleaning of the bathroom. The girls had polished every inch of the cabin spotless, but two scouts needed a last-minute bathroom break just as we were about to lock the front door behind us. As a result, Diane insisted on cleaning the facility one more time herself, just to make sure everything was left germ-free for her generous friend.

Something zoomed vertically a foot in front of my nose.

Crash!

Had I not been staring directly at the empty kitchen, I would have sworn that a dozen ice cubes had just been dumped into the open metal sink. Diane appeared in the hall doorway. Her face was unusually pale.

"What was that?" She looked as if she didn't really want to hear the answer.

I stared at my friend and pointed toward the sink. "Did—did you see that big rock thing zip right in front of my face? It sounded like something fell in the sink, but I'm sure not going to look to see what it is!"

Diane gulped. "Well, I *did* just mop that floor and I hate to get it dirty again…" she mused. "No," she concluded, "I'm going to look in the sink. I can't leave anything broken for Sandy!" Diane slowly moved toward the center of the narrow kitchen and peered into the depths of the double sink. "Now, how the heck did *this* get in here?" Diane held up a tiny cut-glass salt shaker, no bigger than a half-inch tall. We had never seen it before in our lives.

I glanced around at the walls and spied a small curio cabinet lined with a dozen inch-wide squares. Inside each small square stood a little decorative salt or pepper shaker. Only one square stood empty in the direct center of the open cabinet. Beside that empty square stood the pepper mate to the glass salt shaker Diane had just pulled from the sink.

For the past two nights and days, the small cabin had been rocked and joggled by a dozen jumping, yelling, playing Girl Scouts, yet not one of the delicate shakers had moved. Then on a silent Sunday afternoon when I stood motionless beside the kitchen and Diane was enclosed in the back bathroom, a single salt shaker had flown vertically across the kitchen, almost knocked into my nose, and landed six feet away in the middle of the sink…unbroken! Diane and I looked at each other nervously.

"OK…" my friend sighed as she carefully placed the glass shaker back in its proper place on the wall. She turned toward the empty rooms in back of us and addressed the house. "You don't need to tell us twice! We're going! Thank you for a lovely weekend…" Diane was out the front door. Swarms of hungry forest mosquitoes were preferable to salt shaker–throwing ghosts.

I locked the door behind us, but instead of climbing into my Girl Scout stuffed van, I pulled Diane over to the wooden porch swing that hung from a large oak. "I need to tell you about something that happened to me on the first night here." It was time to fess up about the wandering ghost.

"Did you hear those footsteps, too?" My friend was amazed. "I thought that was Molly walking around my room, until I realized that my bedroom door never opened or closed. Those crazy footsteps went right through!"

My older daughter, Erin, wandered up to us. "What are you guys talking about? It's hot in the van, Mom, and we can't roll down the window or the mosquitoes will get in. Aren't we going home now?"

I told my ghost-savvy kid about our weekend adventures with flying salt shakers and wandering footsteps. Erin started laughing.

"Oh, my gosh! Was that what you guys were talking about that first night? I wondered what was going on. My sleeping bag was right in between both of your bedroom doors. I was asleep until I heard Miss Diane yelling inside of her bedroom, 'Molly! Is that you? Go back to bed!' Then, a couple of seconds later, I heard Mom yell from her room, 'Erin! Is that you? Go back to bed!' I started to call out to you guys that Molly and I were in our sleeping bags, but I was afraid that I'd wake everyone else up. I figured you guys were talking in your sleep!" From somewhere inside the very clean cabin, the distant chuckle of a satisfied older woman danced across the wind. Or maybe it was just the mosquitoes.

Orlando, Florida:
Two Years Later (Spring 2009)

A gaggle of Girl Scouts encircled my dining room table like Blackbeard's crew stuck at harbor. Outside, Florida's finest spring season was flinging flowers and bumble bees and sunshine all over the neighborhood…but we were stuck in a troop meeting.

I struggled to keep my scouts' attention while my own spring-fevered mind wandered down the old red brick road and around the sparkling lake…I was getting a bit grumpy. "OK, girls, the quicker we figure out how we're gonna collect supplies to send to that African school, the quicker we can get out of here and do something fun outside. Who has a community service suggestion?"

Eleven exhausted heads plopped on the table in reply. Bonnie had to go to the bathroom. Trudi was hungry. Susie had slipped into a vapid coma ten minutes ago. Rebecca was the only child still able to move: she was busy brushing her blanket of hair, flipping it back and forth like a head-banging Nirvana groupie.

I sighed. "Okay, you guys—focus! Sally, what did you collect this month to send to the Kenya school?"

Sally, who always did her homework, jumped to her feet and grinned like Teddy Roosevelt fresh from the dentist. "Weeeeellllll, as you all know, I placed my collection box at my theatrical singing teacher's studio and I got soooooo many donations that I had to empty it every week! I brought every single item with me, as you can see: I have fourteen large boxes of Crayola crayons, assorted colors; nine spiral-bound notebooks; several packs of college-lined writing paper; one mounted pencil sharpener ...

"Oh. My. Gawd!" Rebecca screamed as if her teeth had fallen out. Her eyeballs bulged as she pointed a shaking finger at the open kitchen archway that she faced across the table. "Miss Vivian! Miss Vivian!"

Rebecca was the troop's beloved Whirling Dervish of Attention. She treated splinters like open heart surgery and wondered why the United Nations didn't regard her opinion as law. Rebecca shrieking at my empty kitchen doorway was just the latest chapter in her hyperactive soap opera.

"Beccy, please sit down and be quiet! Sally has the floor and she's doing a great job reporting on her project."

"B-b-but, Miss Vivian!"

I stood up and pulled on my best Mother Superior scowl. "Rebecca, *sit down and be quiet!*"

Rebecca sat. "OK, but can I please, please, *please* tell you guys what I just saw when Sally is done talking?"

"You may tell us whatever you want to, *after* we finish planning this community service project."

"But, that's gonna take forever! Miss Vivian, you just gotta hear this ..."

Trudi whined for a third snack break. I gave up.

"OK, Beccy..."

The words flew out of the teen's mouth so fast that she beat light speed:

"Omigosh, omigosh, omigosh!" (Deep breath.) "OK, so I was brushing my hair, right? And I flipped my head up to get my hair out of my eyes, right? And I looked straight ahead of me into the kitchen and…omigosh! There was a *man* standing right there in the open doorway *staring* straight at me!"

My daughter Erin and I glanced at each other across the table.

"That was just my dad," Erin suggested with a forced shrug.

"No, it wasn't!" Beccy insisted. "Erin, I know what your dad looks like, and besides, he isn't even here! This man was really tall and looked really, really mean at me and then he vanished! I'm not kidding. He just *disappeared* right in front of me. And he was lookin' only at me with this really creepy stare!"

I gulped. During the years that troop meetings had been held around my dining room table, I had never, ever commented on any of the scouts' suspicions that my lovely old house was haunted. Now, twelve pairs of thrillingly horrified eyes were glued to my face. For the past eight years, these girls had regarded me as more than their troop leader; I was practically their second mother. They knew I would rather drink boiling vinegar than lie to them. What were they going to say to their parents? What was *I* going to say to their parents? My poor daughter, Erin, was about to crawl under the rug. It was tough enough to be fifteen years old, but it was nothing short of cruel and unusual punishment to have to endure that stage of life with a bunch of embarrassing ghosts popping up in front of your friends.

There was nothing else for me to do. I was cornered.

"I'm going to make myself a sandwich."

The girls stared in amazed horror as I marched through the haunted kitchen archway and opened my refrigerator door. In the far corner of the kitchen, a tall shadow bowed slightly toward me. I smiled and considered tossing him a Girl Scout cookie.

EPILOGUE

My stove is very old. It's not as old as my house, but it has a few good years on most of my other appliances. There's nothing outwardly remarkable about it. It has four electric burners on the top and one big front door that opens into the oven, which is eternally in need of cleaning. Most of the time, it's pretty reliable and cooks the way every other normal stove has cooked since someone first stuck a flat stone on top of the local fire pit. The single item that sets it apart from all of the other stoves in the world is its timer.

Most semi-modern cooking devices have a timer: you set it for a certain time and it rings when the time runs out. If you picked the correct amount of time, your cookies are baked but not burnt. My timer, however, is different: if I forget to set it, or even turn it on, it still rings if any food is overdone. I wish the smoke detector on my wall was as trustworthy! Many of my friends are skeptical of my magical timer; some say it's haunted, and a few are even a little envious and wish that they had one, too, but, as far as I know, it is unique to this stove. I have no idea why it does what it does, but after years of trial and error, I've learned to pop open the oven door and turn down the heat whenever I hear that little ringing.

For years, I thought I had the only psychic kitchen timer in the whole, wide world until one morning when I was having coffee with my new friend Dana. At precisely 9:38 a.m., her wall clock suddenly struck the hour. "You have a confused clock!" I logically laughed.

"Um, not really," Dana replied. "Excuse me for a sec. I'd better get my cat inside the house before it rains."

Rain? There wasn't a cloud in the state! "I know this sounds crazy," my friend explained after she had pulled her crabby orange feline through the cat door, "but, whenever that clock chimes on the off-hour, bad weather usually hits soon afterward."

Twenty minutes later, the distant grumble of thunder rattled our coffee cups. Dana smiled. "Told ya so!"

Most people think that all clocks work exactly the same way, and that if yours is different—*really* different— you need to either get it fixed or toss it in the trash. But maybe that clock is just telling us something other than the time. Going through life as a Scottish second sight Ghost Magnet is a lot like wearing a weird watch: sometimes my eyes play tricks on me, but most of the time, I've learned to trust that little buzz that says, "We're not alone right now." I have at least four generations of my Scottish family, alive and otherwise, backing me up on that fact.

For most of my life, I thought this spooky trait was unique to only a few members of my family, until I finally began to run into some other distinctive individuals who had met a few ghosts, too. So, I'm really not all that different, after all. True, I seem to pick up on spirits faster than the average Joe, but there are plenty of gifted people who are much more sensitive than I am. When one of my ultra-clairvoyant colleagues was asked to describe how a ghost looked as opposed to a living human, she replied, "What's the difference? They both look the same to me!" Another of my friends is gifted in psychometry, which is the ability to read the history of certain objects when she holds that object in her hand. Pretty cool! I simply mind my own business and bump into ghosts in most of the places I live or visit…or they bump into me. At this point, dealing with the non-living has become a part of my regular daily life!

Most folks would agree that one of the main goals of every living thing is to avoid death as long as possible. Some have attempted this and, along the way, a few souls—human or otherwise—seem to get stuck somewhere in-between. Maybe that's what happened to the spirits I sense; maybe not. Modern science yearns to find logical explanations for "things that go bump in the night," but the truth is that Shakespeare's Hamlet was right: "There are more things in heaven and earth, Horatio, than are dreamt of in your philosophy."

I guess that's why God made some of us Ghost Magnets.

GET MORE AT LLEWELLYN.COM

Visit us online to browse hundreds of our books and decks, plus sign up to receive our e-newsletters and exclusive online offers.

- • Free tarot readings • Spell-a-Day • Moon phases
- • Recipes, spells, and tips • Blogs • Encyclopedia
- • Author interviews, articles, and upcoming events

GET SOCIAL WITH LLEWELLYN

Find us on
Facebook

www.Facebook.com/LlewellynBooks

Follow us on

www.Twitter.com/Llewellynbooks

GET BOOKS AT LLEWELLYN

LLEWELLYN ORDERING INFORMATION

Order online: Visit our website at www.llewellyn.com to select your books and place an order on our secure server.

Order by phone:
- • Call toll free within the U.S. at 1-877-NEW-WRLD (1-877-639-9753)
- • Call toll free within Canada at 1-866-NEW-WRLD (1-866-639-9753)
- • We accept VISA, MasterCard, and American Express

Order by mail:
Send the full price of your order (MN residents add 6.875% sales tax) in U.S. funds, plus postage and handling to: Llewellyn Worldwide, 2143 Wooddale Drive Woodbury, MN 55125-2989

POSTAGE AND HANDLING:

STANDARD: (U.S. & Canada)
(Please allow 2 business days)
$25.00 and under, add $4.00.
$25.01 and over, FREE SHIPPING.

INTERNATIONAL ORDERS (airmail only):
$16.00 for one book, plus $3.00 for each additional book.

Visit us online for more shipping options. Prices subject to change.

FREE CATALOG!

To order, call
1-877-
NEW-WRLD
ext. 8236
or visit our
website

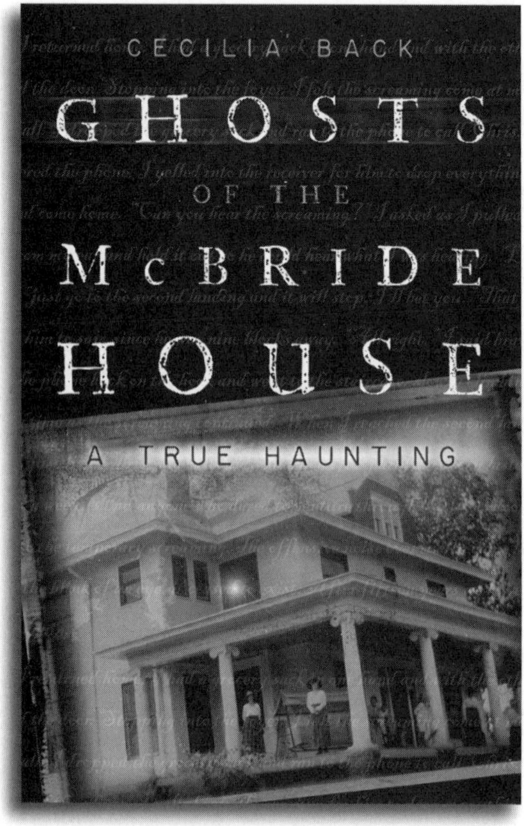
CECILIA BACK
GHOSTS
OF THE
McBRIDE
HOUSE
A TRUE HAUNTING

Ghosts of the McBride House
A True Haunting
Cecilia Back

It took Cecilia Back only a few weeks to confirm that her new home—a Victorian mansion just across the street from a historic military fort—was haunted. But instead of fleeing, the Back family stayed put and gradually got to know their "spirited" residents over the next twenty-five years.

Meet Dr. McBride, the original owner who loves scaring away construction crews and the author's ghost-phobic mother. Try to catch sight of the two spirit children who play with Back's son and daughter and loud, electronic toys in the middle of the night. Each ghost has a personality of its own, including one transient entity whose antics are downright terrifying.

Despite mischievous pranks, such as raucous ghost parties at two a.m., the Back family have come to accept—and occasionally welcome—these unique encounters with the dead.

978-0-7387-1505-6, 216 pp., 5³⁄₁₆ x 8   **$14.95**

To order, call 1-877-NEW-WRLD
Prices subject to change without notice
Order at Llewellyn.com 24 hours a day, 7 days a week!

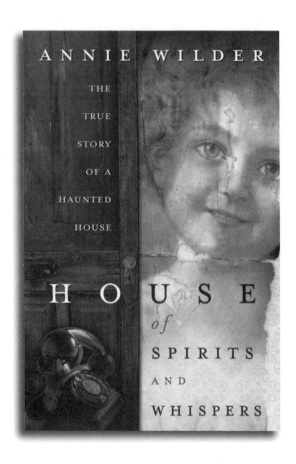

ANNIE WILDER

THE
TRUE
STORY
OF A
HAUNTED
HOUSE

HOUSE
of
SPIRITS
AND
WHISPERS

House of Spirits and Whispers
The True Story of a Haunted House
ANNIE WILDER

Annie Wilder suspected the funky 100-year-old house was haunted when she saw it for the first time. But nothing could have prepared her for the mischievous and downright scary antics that take place once she, her two children, and her cats move into the rundown Victorian home. Disembodied conversation, pounding walls, glowing orbs, and mysterious whispers soon escalate into full-fledged ghostly visits—provoking sheer terror that, over time, transforms into curiosity. Determined to make peace with her spirit guests, she invites renowned clairvoyant Echo Bodine over and learns fascinating details about each of the entities residing there.

Wilder's gripping tale provides a compelling glimpse into the otherworldly nature of the lonely spirits, protective forces, phantom pets, and departed loved ones that occupy her remarkable home.

978-0-7387-0777-8, 192 pp., 6 x 9 **$13.95**

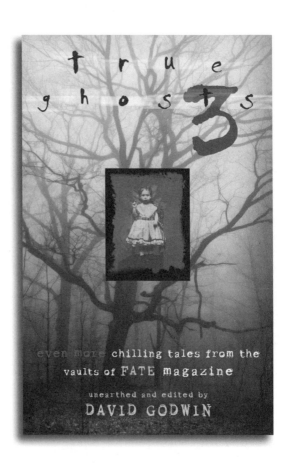

true
ghosts 3

even more chilling tales from the
vaults of FATE magazine

unearthed and edited by
DAVID GODWIN

True Ghosts 3
Even More Chilling Tales
from the Vaults of FATE *Magazine*
Edited by David Godwin

A spirit surgeon repairs a nurse's shattered arm. An Eskimo hunter provides for his family from the great beyond. The fearsome antics of a malevolent entity escalate to physical assault.

Documenting the strange, otherworldly, and truly bizarre since 1948, *FATE* Magazine offers another eye-opening collection of true stories that range from heartwarming to truly terrifying—encounters with departed family members and pets, protective angels and spirit guardians, ghost children, phantom vehicles, poltergeists, and vicious demonic beasts. Dating back to the early 1900s, these vivid eyewitness accounts—including out-of-body experiences, time slips, and dream visitations—offer an unforgettable and spine-tingling glimpse of the great unknown.

978-0-7387-2587-1, 336 pp., 5³⁄₁₆ x 8   **$15.95**

TRUE POLICE STORIES

OF THE

STRANGE & UNEXPLAINED

Detective Sergeant Ingrid P. Dean

FOREWORD BY Kathryn Harwig

True Police Stories of the Strange & Unexplained
Ingrid P. Dean

Divine protection from angels, bizarre synchronistic events, stunning miracles that defy logic. Police officers experience the strange and extraordinary all the time, but rarely talk about it. *True Police Stories of the Strange & Unexplained* offers a rare and gripping glimpse inside their perilous day-to-day lives.

These true, first-hand accounts from law enforcement officials across the nation reveal how intuition, apparitions, UFOs, prophetic dreams, and other forces beyond our understanding have impacted them in the course of duty. From death-defying gun battles to thrilling rescues to heart-searing tragedies, and even a few comical encounters, these truly amazing tales shed light on what our police force faces every day—and expose the fascinating inner lives of the heroic men and women behind the badge.

978-0-7387-2644-1, 288 pp., 5³⁄₁₆ x 8   **$15.95**

Ghost
Hunting

For Beginners

Everything You Need to Know to Get Started

RICH NEWMAN

Ghost Hunting for Beginners
Everything You Need to Know to Get Started
RICH NEWMAN

For the countless fans of ghost hunting TV shows who are itching to get off the couch and track some spirits on their own, professional ghost hunter Rich Newman arms beginners with all they need to start investigating.

Discover proven scientific methods and the latest technology used by the pros. You'll learn about what ghosts are, why hauntings occur, the different types of supernatural phenomena, conducting responsible investigations, forming a team, interacting with spirits, examining evidence—and what not to do when seeking spirits. Peppered with ghost stories from famous cases and the author's own investigations, this book will help you become a true paranormal investigator.

978-0-7387-2696-0, 240 pp., 5³⁄₁₆ x 8 **$14.95**

PARANORMAL OBSESSION

OBSESSION

America's Fascination with
Ghosts & Hauntings, Spooks & Spirits

DEONNA KELLI SAYED

Paranormal Obsession
America's Fascination with Ghosts & Hauntings, Spooks & Spirits
Deonna Kelli Sayed

Why is America so captivated by the unexplained? Far beyond a book of ghost stories, *Paranormal Obsession* offers a unique cultural studies approach to the global phenomena of spirits, ghost hunting, and all things otherworldly.

Providing an insider's view from within the spirit-seeking community, paranormal investigator Deonna Kelli Sayed explores how and why our love of spirits started, how ghosts took over the small screen, the roles of science and religion, our fascination with life after death—and what it all says about American culture.

Weighing perspectives of ghost hunters, religious figures, scientists, academics, parapsychologists, and cast members of the popular TV shows *Ghost Hunters* and *Paranormal State*, this book offers compelling insight into Americans' fixation on ghostly activity. It also highlights the author's paranormal group's investigation of the *USS North Carolina*, the most haunted battleship in the United States.

978-0-7387-2635-9, 264 pp., 6 x 9   **$15.95**

Body, Mind & Spirit / Supernatural

Chilling true stories from an extraordinarily haunted life

Shadowed by the supernatural since childhood, Vivian Campbell has encountered angry wraiths, mischievous child spirits, terrorizing demons, and all sorts of bizarre, unearthly beings. In *Stalked by Spirits*, Vivian relives these thrilling experiences. Over the years, she and her family have suffered violent phantom attacks, received small favors from a little girl ghost, negotiated with a demanding spirit, welcomed back a dearly departed pet, tolerated ghostly attendance at Girl Scout meetings, and even waged hair-raising battles with an evil entity threatening th~~e~~ ~~baby~~ daughter.

Vivian t~~~~ ~~~~ ~~~~ spirit-infested, often beautiful places, ~~from~~ ~~~~ ~~~~ ion in the Tennessee mountains to a century-old college dorm to the beloved Florida home that's been in her family for generations.

Vivian Campbell is a paranormal investigator and sensitive who has lived in haunted houses throughout her life. Her experiences have been included in several books and a television documentary. She continues to live in her creepy·yet much-loved house in central Florida with spirits that have haunted her family for generations.

$15.95 US
$18.50 CAN

Llewellyn Worldwide
www.llewellyn.com
www.facebook.com/LlewellynBooks

ISBN 978-0-7387-2731-8

51595

9 780738 727318